THE CHURCH

WITHOUT

SPOT

OR

WRINKLE

7 STEPS TO BECOMING A PURE & SPOTLESS BRIDE READY FOR THE DAY OF THE LORD

BRONDON MATHIS

Contact info:
Brondon Mathis
614 745-9683, office
816-654-2186, cell
yeshuamovement@gmail.com
facebook/brondonmathis.com

Table of Contents

INTRODUCTION

A Vision of Coming Years of Judgment

The Church without spot or wrinkle is a book on how the church will be prepared as a bride adorned for her husband to partner with the Lord during the unique dynamics of the coming Great and Terrible day of the Lord. The mandate and revelation for this book was given to me on November 11, 2011, (11-11-11.) It was on this date in Detroit Michigan at *"THE CALL Detroit"* - *a 24hr prayer gathering of 40,000 people at Ford Field* - that I was visited by the spirit of God at 3:00 am in the morning with this message and mandate. During this time I was given several messages during a divine visitation from the Lord that I was mandated to write and put in books for a time to come. This book is one of a series of books I've currently published on www.Amazon.com from this visitation from the Lord on 11-11-11.

In this visitation I was given a prophetic word of wisdom for the coming years of 2012-2015, to prepare my heart, life and family for difficult times that are on the horizon in our nation and world. I later realized that it was not just for me and my home, but that it was also a word that I was to begin sharing with the whole body of Christ, helping to prepare the Church for these hard times to come. In this visitation God began to reveal to me what to do to be covered, protected, and provided for supernaturally during systemic shakings and so-called *"Natural disasters."* Many in the body of Christ believed and prophesied that 2011 would begin these coming judgments, unusual weather patterns and drought like conditions, causing economic, financial and relational shakings because of the prophetic significance of this year of 2011.

The Prophetic Symbolism of 2011

The number 11 in numerology means chaos, disorder, and judgment. The number 11 three times on the Gregorian calendar only comes once in a hundred years. Many prophetic voices had prophesied that 11 three times on the Gregorian calendar in the day, month, and year, could signal the release of judgment, chaos and disorder in our society. This 24hr prayer meeting in Detroit on November 11, 2011, was focused on how to turn or lessen this judgment on our nation here in the United States by praying in accordance with Joel 2, in Detroit Michigan, one of the most economically depressed cities in the United States. Based on what was revealed to me to prepare my own life, family and City in this visitation at 3:00am in the morning, and what we've seen happening in our nation since that time, I believe 2012 could have possibly began the birth pangs and the forerunner of what the bible calls *"The Great and Terrible Day of the Lord,"* and the *CALL DETROIT* was a prescription of how the body of Christ is to respond – *with 24 hr Prayer Vigils* - during coming economic and financial shakings that challenge the infrastructures of cities throughout the nations of the world.

The Drought of 2012 and Financial Collapse of Detroit of 2013

We now know at the time of the writing of the second edition of this book in 2013, written from this visitation, that the following summer of 2012 was the worst drought to hit the United States of America in over 100 years. This drought was precipitated by temperatures of 110 degrees throughout the country. We also now know that the City of Detroit, in 2013, became the first major city in U.S. History to file for Bankruptcy. Below is an excerpt from www.CBSnews.com

Once the very symbol of American industrial might, Detroit became the biggest U.S. city to file for bankruptcy Thursday, its finances ravaged and its neighborhoods hollowed out by a long, slow decline in population and auto manufacturing.

The filing, which had been feared for months, put the city on an uncertain course that could mean laying off municipal employees, selling off assets, raising fees and scaling back basic services such as trash collection and snow plowing, which have already been slashed.

The result is a city where whole neighborhoods are practically deserted and basic services cut off in places. Looming over the crumbling landscape is a budget deficit believed to be more than $380 million and long-term debt that could be as much as $20 billion.

The Spirit of the Lord began revealing to me several decades ago, in 1992, that our society and economic system (a debtor society) is headed in our nation for a complete economic and financial collapse like that which happened in Detroit. I believe this fallout could be precipitated by a similar financial collapse as was seen in Detroit, from out of control debt. If our country's debt continues to escalate as it has over the last 5 years, it would be what compounds our economic, financial problems in our economy, pushing it over that proverbial fiscal cliff talked about so much by the legislators in our country in the latter part of 2012. In my book, *"My Money is Restored,"* I share what we must do to prepare financially, as well as to prepare cities of refuge in key cities around this nation that will have storehouses of food, and 24/7 houses of prayer for believers to look to God and one another for sustenance, supply and spiritual and natural food during this Economic, Financial and food fallout. The body of Christ will need to be purified and cleansed to return to Acts 4 communities where we have all things in common and there is none that lack among us.

> *Act 4:31* **And when they had prayed, the place was shaken where they were assembled together**; *and they were all filled with the Holy Ghost, and they spake the word of God with boldness. 32 And the multitude of them that believed were of one heart and of one soul: neither said any of them that ought of the things which he possessed was his own; but they had all things common. 33. And with great power gave the apostles witness of the resurrection of the Lord Jesus: and great grace was upon them all.* **34. Neither was there any among them that lacked: for as many as were possessors of lands or houses sold them, and brought the prices of the things that were sold, 35 And laid them down at the apostles' feet: and distribution was made unto every man according as he had need.**

The Church without Spot or Wrinkle

I believe that God is releasing wisdom into the earth for His church in preparation for this day. I believe God is positioning His church now, to be a pure and spotless bride to partner with His end-time plan to transition the earth to the Day of the Lord. To do this God is releasing revelation from His word to sanctify and cleanse His church, that it might be a glorious church, not having spot or wrinkle or any such thing. Ephesians 5:26, 27 says it like this;

> *That he might sanctify and cleanse it with the washing of water by the word, 27 That he might*

> *present it to himself a glorious church, not having spot, or wrinkle, or any such thing; but that it should be holy and without blemish.*

The Final Expression of His Church as a House of Prayer for All Nations

One such expression of God's wisdom and revelation for the cleansing of His church is going to be the coming forth of the original, final and eternal expression of his Church as a House of Prayer for all nations. During this day of shaking and judgment of the nations, those that come to his holy mountain - *the place of prayer* - will be covered, protected and provided for in his house of prayer. (Isaiah 2:2-5 Isaiah 56:6-8). This coming day of the Lord is going to coincide with this final restoration movement and expression of Prayer being returned and restored to our foremost identity in the Church.

Since 1525 and the reformation of Martin Luther the church of Jesus Christ has been in a process of restoration of its original teachings and purpose in the earth. Below is a comprehensive list of the various restorative movements that have taken place in the church of Jesus Christ since the 1500's:

- *The Protestant Movement - Saved by faith (1525)*
- *The Evangelical Movement - Baptism in water (1800's),*
- *The Pentecost Revival - Baptism w/the Holy Ghost, with evidence of speaking in tongues (1900's),*
- *The Healing Revival –Healings, Signs, Wonders and Miracles (1949),*
- *The Charismatic movement – The Gifts of the Holy Ghost reaching across denominational lines (1960's),*
- *The Word of Faith movement – The Teaching of the word of God for Prevailing Faith (1980's)*

- *The Mega Church movement – The Restoration of the Five-fold Ministry Gifts (1990's), and;*
- *The Prayer Movement – The restoring of the Tabernacle of David expression of the Church, with a day and night prayer & worship, city-wide, 24/7, expression of the Church in regions of the earth. (2000's).*

I believe that the Prayer movement in the earth is the last restoration movement in the Church before the coming of the Lord. Right before Jesus returns the original expression of the House of God as a House of Prayer for All Nations, and the Tabernacle of David for Prayer and worship day and night will be restored as the final expression of the church at the end of the age.

> *Act 15:16 After this I will return, and will build again the tabernacle of David, which is fallen down; and I will build again the ruins thereof, and I will set it up: 17 That the residue of men might seek after the Lord, and all the Gentiles, upon whom my name is called, says the Lord, who doeth all these things.*

For this to happen the Church of Jesus Christ is going to have to be washed, cleansed and purified from her man-made religious, doctrinal and theological biases of the past centuries, which has led to the compromising, sinful, and passive expression of the Church of the 21st Century. The Church without spot or wrinkle will only be seen when we return to the Revelation of Jesus Christ and build our house upon the rock of this Man and His Message to the Churches of Asia in preparation for His coming day, called the Day of the Lord. Within the pages of this book is a 7 step breakdown of each message revealed to John of Jesus Christ and His ideal image of His Church, given to the 7 churches of Asia from Revelation 2 and 3. These Churches in the book of the Revelation are a snapshot of the state of the Universal Church at the end of the age, and these 7 messages are how the end-time Church will be transformed to become His bride without Spot of Wrinkle or any such thing, partnering with Him at the end of the age, to transition the earth to the age to come. A Revelation of Jesus the glorified Christ, in chapter 1, caused John to get a vision of the Church in chapters 2 and 3 *Without Spot or Wrinkle or any such thing*. These 7 prophetic messages will wash the 21st century Church from her compromise, sin and doctrinal error, and prepare her to partner with Jesus in His world-wide action plan related to His second coming.

CHAPTER 1

THE DAY OF THE LORD IN THE BOOK OF THE REVELATION OF JESUS CHRIST

"The sun will be turned to darkness and the moon to blood before the coming of the Great and Terrible day of the Lord." Acts 2:20

What is this Day of the Lord? Not too many believers in Christendom have an adequate understanding of what the Day of the Lord is. Many in the body of Christ are unaware of the unique dynamics of this day and what our actual preparation for this day entails. The day of the Lord is most talked about in the book of Zephaniah, Malachi, Joel, and the Revelation of Jesus Christ. However Peter, in quoting the book of Joel describes this day in correlation with the spirit of God that will be poured out on all flesh in the last days in Acts 2:20, saying, *"The sun will be turned to darkness and the moon to blood before the coming of the Great and Terrible day of the Lord."*

There are two main characteristics of this day of the Lord. It will be a Great day, but it will also be a terrible day.

GREAT DAY - The Day of the Lord will have "great" attributes and characteristics for those that respond to Him as He releases the greatest manifestation of His power in natural human history. He is going to change the understanding and expression of Christianity in the whole earth in one generation. It will be the greatest time for the church in history.

VERY TERRIBLE DAY - The day of the Lord will also be the most severe time of God's judgment ever on earth since the beginning of human history. (Rev. 6-20)

...Yet once more I shake not only the earth, but heaven also...that the things, which cannot be shaken, remain. (Heb 12, 26-27) The four angels, who had been prepared for the house and day....were released to kill a third of mankind. (Rev. 9:15-16)

There has never been a day like this before on the face of the earth. Not in power or pressure. Not the cloud and pillar of fire of Moses in the wilderness. Not World War II, where 50 million died, not Hitler, Stalin, not even the Pentecostal Revivals of Azusa or the Day of Pentecost.

I will pour My Spirit out on all flesh.... I will show wonders in the heavens and in the earth: Blood, fire and pillars of smoke......(Joel 2:28-30)

For there will be great tribulation, such has not been since the beginning of the world until this time, no, nor ever shall be. (Matt 24.21)

The great and terrible dimensions of the Day of the Lord will both increase dramatically the closer we get to the return of Jesus and will find their fullest expressions in the final 3 ½ years of natural human history. I believe this year could be a warning year for the church to receive an urgency and fervency to get in the prayer position to be pre-prayer-ed (prayed up) for this day. I believe in 2012 he began positioning in his end-time Church, Josephs, Daniels and many end-time forerunners to rise up and begin to declare and pre-prayer with wisdom, revelation (dreams & visions) and wealth, for the preservation of His people during the coming of the Great and Terrible day of the Lord.

14

In this visitation on the date 11-11-11 in Detroit Michigan at *THE CALL DETROIT*, the Spirit of God spoke to me and told me that the Day of Lord is fast approaching, and that 11-11-11 signals a pivotal time of coming together in the church across racial and socio-economic divides to begin seeking the face of My Son for the release of divine *Love, Peace, Reconciliation, Protection and Provision* towards preparation for the coming of this day. He further said that the church of this generation is not ready for the unique dynamics of this day. He said that this day will cause offense and a falling away of many that name the name of Christ if they are not adequately prepared in prayer. He said if my people don't clearly understand this coming day and adequately PRE-PRAYER for it, my church will not be able to endure and stand in this day.

> *Blow the trumpet in Zion, sanctify a fast, call a solemn assembly: Gather the people, sanctify the congregation, assemble the elders, gather the children, and those that suck the breasts: let the bridegroom go forth of his chamber, and the bride out of her closet. Let the priests, the ministers of the LORD, weep between the porch and the altar, and let them say, Spare thy people, O LORD (Joel 2:15-17).*

Sacred Assemblies Coming to the Church

Sacred Assemblies like the 24hr Call Detroit are God's prescribed method to either avert the judgment completely, or lessen it in a geographical region, or prepare a generation to stand without offense in the midst of the economic, environmental, and military crisis that are clearly seen in Joel and passages that clearly articulate the conditions of the end of the age. Prayer meetings are God's remedy of response to impending judgment. I believe this Detroit Call to 24 hours of prayer, as well as many of the other prayer meetings on this date in that year was given, not to be a one-time event, but as a prescription of what we will do during the time of the *Day of the Lord*. God's remedy for preservation, protection and provision for his people during this coming day, is night and day prayer meetings in the nations of the earth.

Word of the Lord Given During a Visitation the Morning of the Call Detroit

In this visitation, He took me to the book of The Revelation of Jesus Christ and took me to Chapters 1 – 3 and showed me what John actually saw when he was transported by the Spirit to the end of the age. John actually saw the Day of the Lord. He was transported there by the Spirit – *I was In the Spirit on the Lord's Day…..* Rev 1:10. John saw two things.

1. The first thing John was shown was the Glorified Christ.
2. The second thing John saw was the Church of that day.

I believe that day is this day, and the distinguishing trait of messengers in the last day's right before the coming day of the Lord will be encounters with the Glorified Christ. Messengers at the end of the age will first be marked with an encounter with the Christ of the message before they are given a message to speak for Christ. John saw the Glorified Christ in Revelation 1, and was given messages for His church to prepare them for the day of the Lord. These messages given to the 7 churches of Asia were also given to prepare the *Universal Church* at the end of the age to be positioned to model what the church should look like, right before the coming day of the Lord. If we would receive the message of the angel of the Lord and repent, we would be positioned to partner in prayer in the earth, with Christ's prayers and the prayers of the saints in heaven to administer justice and judgment in the earth during this day.

16

> *Rev 1:10 I was in the Spirit on the Lord's Day, and heard behind me a great voice, as of a trumpet;*

The Lord's Day is the day when the Lord will judge and cleanse the earth from sin and evil and release his spirit to gather his people together for the setting up of his kingdom on the earth. Malachi, Joel and the book of Acts calls this day, *"The Great and Terrible Day of the Lord."* It's followed by the question, *"Who shall be able to stand?"* This is what John was saying and seeing in the book of the Revelation, when he says, *"I was in the spirit on the LORD'S DAY."* He was actually saying, *"I saw it as if I was there,* because I was there.....in the spirit." He then begins to describe a man (Jesus, the Glorified Christ) and a message that was given him to write and speak to the church right before and during that day, preparing the church for the day of the Lord. It's this message that the book of The Revelation of Jesus Christ represents. It is a message to the church right before this day that John saw, to position her to be able to stand in that day.

I heard behind me a great voice, as of a trumpet. Rev. 1:10

The word *"voice"* is the Greek word, *"fo-nay,"* which is where we get the English word *"Phone,"* and it means; **a *tone* (articulate, bestial or artificial**); by implication **an *address*** (for any purpose), ***saying* or *language:*** - noise, sound, voice.

I believe John was not only saying that he was there during the day of the Lord in the Spirit, but I believe he very well could have been describing here how the message was being transmitted to the church at the end of the age. During this day he heard a great address taking place, a voice being sounded as a trumpet. Could it be that this voice John heard as a trumpet, which means in the Greek phōnē, was John's only way of describing that this message was being transmitted through I-Phones? In other words, John was in Spirit at the end of times seeing the day of the Lord, trying to describe in his limited understanding what the mode of communication was at the end of the age, and during this time the great messages and addresses of the Lord were going all over the world at once, being heard and seen loud and clear, coming through phones that everyone had access to. If the trumpet of John's day was the I-Phones of this day it would definitely describe the day we live in now with cell phones with the ability to receive video messages.

As of a trumpet:

The word trumpet in the Greek is the word sal- pinx, which comes from a word that means: *sainō sah'ee-no, meaning to wag (as a dog its tail fawningly), that is, (generally) to shake (figuratively disturb): - move. WHICH IS THE WORD SEIO; si'-o; apparently a primary verb; to rock (vibrate, properly sideways or to and fro), that is, (generally) to agitate (in any direction; cause to tremble); figuratively to throw into a tremor (of fear or concern): - move, quake, shake.*

This word trumpet is where we get the English word seismic; which means, shaking, movement, vibration. These great voices, messages, sermons, or addresses were so great that they caused spiritual and literal shakings, or tremors, like earthquakes that begin in a central location where there is a fault line and expands to effect the earth thousands of miles away. During this day of the Lord these great messages went forth with great reverberation, shaking, disturbance, and agitation. It wasn't a nice little sermon that was embraced by everyone, but it was seen and heard by everyone and it caused great agitation, shaking, and disturbance.

Eight Things we can do from Rev. 1:6-19 to be positioned To Receive the Messages of the 7 Churches

*Rev 1:4 John to the seven churches which are in Asia: **Grace be unto you, and peace,** from him which is, and which was, and which is to come; and from the seven Spirits which are before his throne;*

*Rev 1:5 **And from Jesus Christ, who is the faithful witness,** and the first begotten of the dead, and the prince of the kings of the earth. **Unto him that loved us, and washed us from our sins in his own blood,** 6 And hath made us kings and priests unto God and his Father; to him be glory and dominion forever and ever. Amen.*

7 Behold, he cometh with clouds; and every eye shall see him, and they also which pierced him: and all kindreds of the earth shall wail because of him. Even so, Amen. 8 I am Alpha and Omega, the beginning and the ending, says the Lord, which is, and which was, and which is to come, the Almighty.

*9 I John, who also am your brother, and companion in tribulation, and in the kingdom and patience of Jesus Christ, was in the isle that is called Patmos, for the word of God, and for the testimony of Jesus Christ. 10 **I was in the Spirit on the Lord's day, and heard** behind me a great voice, as of a trumpet,*

11 Saying, I am Alpha and Omega, the first and the last: and, What you see, write in a book, and send it unto the seven churches which are in Asia; unto Ephesus, and unto Smyrna, and unto Pergamos, and unto Thyatira, and unto Sardis, and unto

Philadelphia, and unto Laodicea. 12 ***And I turned to see the voice that spoke with me. And being turned****, I saw seven golden candlesticks;*

13 ***And in the midst of the seven candlesticks one like unto the Son of man****, clothed with a garment down to the foot, and girt about the paps with a golden girdle. 14 His head and his hairs were white like wool, as white as snow; and his eyes were as a flame of fire; 15 And his feet like unto fine brass, as if they burned in a furnace; and his voice as the sound of many waters.*

16 And he had in his right hand seven stars: and out of his mouth went a sharp two-edged sword: and his countenance was as the sun shines in his strength. 17 And when I saw him, I fell at his feet as dead. And he laid his right hand upon me, saying unto me, Fear not; I am the first and the last: 18 I am he that lives, and was dead; and, behold, I am alive for evermore, Amen; and have the keys of hell and of death.

19 ***Write the things which thou hast seen, and the things which are, and the things which shall be hereafter;*** *20 The mystery of the seven stars which thou sawest in my right hand, and the seven golden candlesticks. The seven stars are the angels of the seven churches: and the seven candlesticks which thou saw are the seven churches.*

From these verses I received 8 things the church must do to position her to receive the messages of the 7 Churches.

1. Receive the Grace and Peace that comes from a revelation of He, which is (presently), which was (In generations past) and which is to come (In the future). - Rev. 1:4
2. Receive the spirit of faithfulness, to be a faithful witness. - Rev. 1:5
3. Receive the love of God that washes us from our sins in his blood. - Rev. 1:5
4. Be spirit conscious to live and walk in the spirit as we see the day of the Lord approaching – Rev 1:10
5. Receive the spirit of repentance causing us to turn (repent) see and follow the voice that speaks with us. - Rev. 1:12
6. Encounter the spirit of God, in order to receive the end-time revelation of Jesus the Glorified Christ. – Rev 1:13-16
7. Receive a Prophetic spirit to show unto his servants, the Church, the things which must shortly come to pass; - Rev. 1:17
8. Receive a revelation of Christ's Church as we see Him standing in the midst of the candlesticks and lamp stands, purifying her to be without spot, wrinkle or any such thing. - Rev.1:12-1

Prayers of Repentance & Intercessory Identification Representing the Church at the end of the age from the 7 churches of Asia

The Spirit of God then gave me 7 prayers to pray of repentance in my heart for my life, and family and for intercessory identification for his church, representing this generation of believers, from the 7 churches of Asia in Revelation 2 and 3. Below are the 7 prayers of repentance he gave me to pray on 11-11-11 at the 24hr Detroit Call Prayer Gathering.

The 7 Churches of Asia - Revelation 2 & 3

Write the things which thou hast seen, and the things which are, and the things which shall be hereafter; Rev 1:19

1. The Church Of Ephesus. Rev. 2:4 Nevertheless I have somewhat against thee, because thou hast left thy first love. **Prayer of Repentance:** *Jesus, I repent for leaving my first love (An intimate relationship with Jesus Christ). I will return to intimacy with you, loving you with all my heart, mind, soul and strength, spending time with you as my first defense against the temptation to work or serve for your acceptance, and against the temptation of the lust of the flesh, the lust of the eyes, and the pride of life. Lord, I turn back to seeking your face. I turn to studying the bridal paradigm of your heart and emotions of love for us as your bride found in the Song of Solomon. I covenant to keep a sacred charge for personal prayer times and corporate prayer times in prayer room gatherings in your body, to intercede for your church to return the first commandment to first place in our midst.*

2. The Church Of Smyrna - Rev 2:10 Fear none of those things which thou shall suffer: behold, the devil shall cast some of you into prison, that ye may be tried; and ye shall have tribulation ten days: be thou faithful unto death, and I will give thee a crown of life**. Prayer of Repentance:** *Jesus, I repent for the fear of suffering tribulation and turn to the faithfulness of Christ unto death. (Matt 16:20). Lord, I turn to living and studying to have a mind that is girt with the sufferings of Christ, desiring the fellowship of Christ's sufferings, over the 21st century gospel of comfort and convenience. (1 Peter 4:1-12)*

3. The Church Of Pergamos – Rev 2:14 But I have a few things against thee, because thou hast there them that hold the doctrine of Balaam, who taught Balac to cast a stumbling block before the children of Israel, to eat things sacrificed unto idols, and to commit fornication. **Prayer of Repentance:** *Jesus, I repent for allowing the false doctrine of Balaam - (fornication in the church) to operate in my life. This is the toleration of fornication through the teaching of the Nicoliatans which taught a perversion of the doctrine of liberty, along with Antinomianism, which is the belief that the gospel frees us from obedience to specific moral standards, since we believe that salvation is a gift by faith through grace. Therefore we don't need to repent. <u>Lord, I turn from the spirit of Balaam, eyes of Adultery, and fornication in the church, to spirit of Holiness and sanctification.</u>*

4. The Church Of Thyatira – Rev 2:20 Notwithstanding I have a few things against thee, because thou suffers that woman Jezebel, which calls herself a prophetess, to teach and to seduce my servants to commit fornication, and to eat things sacrificed unto idols. **Prayer of Repentance:** *Jesus, I repent for allowing the spirit of Jezebel to operate in my life. (Worshipping false gods of immorality and sorcery) This happens as we look to satisfy the desire for sexual intimacy and spiritual power unlawfully, through sexual immorality and the worship of demon spirits, through the worship of position and authority in his body, the church. These spirits are manifested in the world through drugs, illicit sex and all types of counterfeit power surges, and in the Church it can come on us as a result of preaching, and teaching as a Pastor or leader in Christ's body with the wrong motives, and heart. This is produced many times through a spirit of performance in the church, as well as assuming counterfeit authority. This spirit is also produced through lusting after position in society (political office, etc), and doing whatever is necessary to obtain those offices and positions. <u>Lord I turn from looking to vain and worthless things to satisfy a desire for illegitimate intimacy. I turn from looking to position and authority in ministry, looking for success and fulfillment through leading and building your Church with the wrong motives. I turn to seeking purity of motives and morality,</u>*

taking a purity covenant with you, and with my wife and children as my accountability partners.

5. The Church of Sardis – Rev 3:2 Be watchful, and strengthen the things which remain, that are ready to die: for I have not found thy works perfect before God. 3 Remember therefore how thou hast received and heard, and hold fast, and repent. If therefore thou shalt not watch, I will come on thee as a thief, and thou shalt not know what hour I will come upon thee. **Prayer of Repentance:** *Jesus, I repent for not watching in prayer to strengthen the things that remain, allowing the thief to steal our doctrines and faith with the various teachings that seek to avoid persecution. Lord, I turn to the study of these doctrines and teachings of the end-times that I have let slip, and commit my life to teach and preach what the bible teaches about the coming of the Lord as Bridegroom, King and Judge.*

6. The Church of Philadelphia – Rev 3:7 And to the angel of the church in Philadelphia write; These things says, he that is holy, he that is true, he that hath the key of David, he that opens, and no man shuts; and shuts, and no man opens; 8 I know thy works: behold, I have set before thee an open door, and no man can shut it: for thou hast a little strength, and hast kept my word, and hast not denied my name. **Prayer of Repentance**: *Jesus, I repent for not pursuing a heart after God and prayer as David for the keys for opening of doors and windows in heaven. I commit to this 24/7 paradigm of the key of David as revealed to the church of Philadelphia. This church was given the keys of David to open a door that is shut, and shut doors that should not be opened. Lord, I commit to rebuilding the Tabernacle of David as your end-time expression of your church as The House of Prayer for all Nations. I commit to establish 24/7 places of worship & prayer in the cities of the earth, culminating in Jerusalem. This is what will enable the church to resist the compromises and the sins represented in the churches of Asia, and be able to stand before the Lord to receive* *the seven spirits of God and strength to endure the things that will come in the days ahead right before and during the Day of the Lord.*

7. The Church of Laodicea – Rev 3:15 I know thy works, that thou art neither cold nor hot: I would thou wert cold or hot. 16 So then because thou art lukewarm, and neither cold nor hot, I will spue thee out of my mouth. 17 Because thou sayest, I am rich, and increased with goods, and have need of nothing; and knowest not that thou art wretched, and miserable, and poor, and blind, and naked: **Prayer of Repentance:** *Jesus, I repent for being made lukewarm (through false and perverted doctrines of prosperity.) Lord, I turn from prosperity for our own benefit, or to make ourselves look appealing and desirable to the world, and I commit to give my heart to you as a living sacrifice, and make a vow to you to offer my money to you for the building of your house of prayer, and cities of refuge throughout this nation and world .*

These are the 7 prayers of repentance and intercessory identification I was instructed to pray on this day in November 2011. These are also the prayers I feel the body of Christ should focus on as we see tremors of this day approaching. In Chapters 3 thru 9, in **The 7 Steps to Purity in the Church,** I will expand on these 7 churches and their shortcomings and look to identify areas where the Universal Church at the end of the age can be positioned to be purified as a bride without spot or wrinkle. Then I will give you an opportunity to pray these same prayers at the end of each **Purity Step** at the end of each of these seven chapters on the 7 Churches. I believe these 7 prayers will position you or your family, church or ministry to become a pure and spotless bride, without spot or wrinkle or any such thing.

CHAPTER 2

HE THAT HATH AN EAR TO HEAR.......
The Purifying Of the 21st Century Church through the Messages to the 7 Churches Of Asia

⁷ He who has an ear, let him hear what the Spirit says to the churches. (Rev. 2:7)

In the last days, Jesus is going to release to his church a hearing ear like no other time in church history, so that he that hath an ear to hear will be able to hear what the Spirit is saying to His church. 8 times in the gospels and 8 times in the book of the revelation Jesus said.......*he that hath an ear to hear let him hear what the spirit says to the church.* Seeing and hearing in the spirit is what's going to purify His church for the unique dynamics of the end-times, and the coming of the Lord. It's through this hearing ear of the prophetic that the church will be cleansed. The prophetic dimension comes not only to bring direction but it comes to bring correction. Correction must come before direction. When the Lord becomes our Shepherd again in his church, Psalm 23:3 says, *Thy Rod (correction) and thy Staff (direction, and protection) will comfort us* The word comfort in the Hebrew text is the word na^cham, which not only means to pity, console, and ease, but it also means to repent. When the Lord becomes our Shepherd, his rod, his correction and his staff, direction and protection will cause us to repent and be led by the spirit. With the rod of correction those that know the voice of their shepherd will repent of those things that the spirit reveals and receive comfort as a part and parcel of the prophetic anointing that comes to purify, purge and process us through the wilderness to the promised land of green pastures. This is what the process of purifying will produce. This process was seen by

Jesus in correcting the churches of Asia in John's Revelation of Jesus to the seven churches.

He Who Has an Ear Let Him Hear: 5 Implications

As I stated above, the exhortation that Jesus repeated the most in His earthly ministry was the call to have ears to hear what the Spirit is saying. This is written 16 times (8x in the Gospels and 8x in Revelation (Mt. 11:15; 13:9, 43; Mk. 4:9, 23; 7:16; Lk. 8:8; 14:35; Rev. 2:7, 11, 17, 29; 3:6, 13, 22; 13:9).

> ^{7} *He who has an ear, let him hear what the Spirit says to the churches. (Rev. 2:7)*

First, it signaled that the truth being proclaimed was *extremely important to Jesus*.

Second, Jesus is saying that *there is more than* what is obvious. He is calling us to pursue the deeper truth being set before us and not to be content to understand only what is on the surface.

Third, it takes the *supernatural help of the Holy Spirit* to grasp it. The unaided mind of even a devoted believer will not be able to automatically comprehend the truth being set forth. Jesus is making it clear that it is beyond our natural ability. Jesus wants us to ask the Spirit for help.

Fourth, each time Jesus spoke this exhortation in Revelation it was about their *eternal rewards and destiny*. He warned them and us to have ears to hear because it takes supernatural insight to grasp them. When reading each reward, pray; "Lord, show me more".

Fifth, it takes a *focused determination* to lay hold of the truths being referred to. We do not automatically respond in a deep and sustained way to them. It will take a tenacious commitment to maintain these truths in our lives long-term because of our propensity to lose touch with them.

Jesus started by speaking to individuals ("he" who has an ear) then changed to addressing a group (the "churches"). There is an individual and a corporate response that the Spirit desires. Jesus was the only one in the NT to give this exhortation. He echoed Moses who called Israel to "hear" meaning to "have ears to hear" (Deut. 6:4-5) and the Father (Ps. 45:10).

> [4] *Hear, O Israel: The LORD our God, the LORD is one! 5 You shall love the LORD your God with all your heart, with all your soul, and with all your strength. (Deut. 6:4-5)*

A Revelation of the Glorified Christ to His Church

The book of the Revelation is called the "revelation of Jesus" because it reveals His heart, power and leadership.

> [1] *The Revelation of Jesus Christ, which God gave Him (Jesus) to show His servants. (Rev. 1:1)*

The theme of the Revelation is Jesus returning to take leadership of the earth in partnership with His people to reap a harvest of souls (Rev. 7:9) and replace all governments (Rev. 11:15; 19:15-16).

> [7] *Behold, He is coming with clouds, and every eye will see Him... (Rev. 1:7)*

Rev. 2-3: Jesus gives us the clearest picture of what He wants in the Church in His seven letters where He exhorts believers to be over comers. Rev. 2-3 is key to forming the end-time prayer and prophetic movement. Jesus will come ONLY in context to a prepared Bride in unity with the Spirit and anointed in prayer to release God's glory on earth and to release the Tribulation to confront darkness.

> [7] *For the marriage of the Lamb has come, and His wife has made herself ready. (Rev. 19:7)*

29

> ^{17} *The Spirit and the Bride say, "Come!" (Rev. 22:17)*

> ^{4} *The prayers of the saints, ascended before God...5 Then the angel took the censer, filled it with fire from the altar, and threw it to the earth... (Rev. 8:4-5)*

The Jn. 14:12 prayer anointing of *"greater works than these shall we do,"* involves the miracles of Exodus and Acts being combined and multiplied on a global level to loose revival and the Tribulation and to bind the Antichrist.

> *Most assuredly, I say to you, he who believes in Me, the works that I do he will do also; and greater works than these he will do, because I go to My Father. (Jn. 14:12)*

> *On this rock I will build My church, and the gates of Hades shall not prevail against it. 19 And I will give you the keys of the kingdom of heaven, and whatever you bind on earth will be bound in heaven, and whatever you loose on earth will be loosed in heaven. (Mt. 16:18-19)*

As Jesus revealed himself in his glorified state to John the Revelator, Jesus is going to reveal himself to his church in the 21st century to purify and prepare His church for the unique dynamics of the end-times and the coming of the Lord. Hearing from and seeing the glorified Christ is the prerequisite for the Church receiving purity and positioning to be prepared as a bride for her husband, not having spot, wrinkle, blemish or any such thing. Her purity is going to come as she is ushered into the presence of the Christ of the lamp stands and are shown things that are, was and are to come. The Church of the 21st century that gets a revelation of Jesus Christ, like was given to John, will see and hear things from the seven Spirits of God which are before the throne

30

Rev 1:1 The Revelation of Jesus Christ, which God gave unto him, to show unto his servants things which must shortly come to pass; and he sent and signified it by his angel unto his servant John: 2 Who bare record of the word of God, and of the testimony of Jesus Christ, and of all things that he saw. 3 Blessed is he that reads, and they that hear the words of this prophecy, and keep those things which are written therein: for the time is at hand. 4 John to the seven churches which are in Asia: Grace be unto you, and peace, from him which is, and which was, and which is to come; and from the seven Spirits which are before his throne; 5 And from Jesus Christ, who is the faithful witness, and the first begotten of the dead, and the prince of the kings of the earth. Unto him that loved us, and washed us from our sins in his own blood, 6 And hath made us kings and priests unto God and his Father; to him be glory and dominion forever and ever. Amen.

A Vision of the Church without Spot or Wrinkle

What John saw of Jesus in chapter 1 of the revelation caused John to get a revelation of the church in chapter 2 the way Jesus created it to be, without spot, or wrinkle or any such thing, holy and without blemish. John received the word that would wash the church from her compromise, sin, doctrinal error, and her weaknesses. The first things John saw after he was translated by the Spirit to the Lord's Day was Jesus revealed in the seven golden candlesticks. The seven golden candlesticks represent the church as the light of the world. The seven candlesticks also represent the outpour of the Holy Spirit in seven dimensions that will cause the church to maneuver through the unique dynamics of the end-times. When the church becomes a house of Prayer and begins to

31

hear and see in the spirit, they will begin to hear the voice as a trumpet that will signal a shift and a pouring out of His spirit to bring light, and illumination to the church.

> *Rev 1:10 I was in the Spirit on the Lord's day, and heard behind me a great voice, as of a trumpet, 11 Saying, I am Alpha and Omega, the first and the last: and, What thou seest, write in a book, and send it unto the seven churches which are in Asia; unto Ephesus, and unto Smyrna, and unto Pergamos, and unto Thyatira, and unto Sardis, and unto Philadelphia, and unto Laodicea.12 And I turned to see the voice that spake with me. And being turned, I saw seven golden candlesticks;*

The Seven Golden Candlesticks –Seven Spirits of God to lead the church through tribulation

The seven golden candlesticks represents the seven spirits of God which will be poured out on the church (the perfected body of Christ) that will cause the church of the 21st century to be able to operate in and through persecution in the end-times, causing her to thrive not just survive, causing her to be raised up, not brought down, to come out victorious, not be overcome or defeated by the enemy. These seven spirits of God that will be seen by the Church is what will cause the church to transition into her end-time and eternal destiny as a House of Prayer for all nations. These seven spirits seen by John, with Jesus standing in the midst of His church, are recorded in Isaiah 11: 2

> *Isa 11:2 And the spirit of the LORD shall rest upon him, the spirit of wisdom and understanding, the spirit of counsel and might, the spirit of knowledge and of the fear of the LORD; 3 And shall make him of quick understanding in the fear of the LORD: and*

he shall not judge after the sight of his eyes, neither reprove after the hearing of his ears: 4 But with righteousness shall he judge the poor, and reprove with equity for the meek of the earth: and he shall smite the earth with the rod of his mouth, and with the breath of his lips shall he slay the wicked. 5 And righteousness shall be the girdle of his loins, and faithfulness the girdle of his reins.

1. The Spirit of the Lord - Jesus Christ
2. The Spirit of Wisdom
3. The Spirit of Understanding
4. The Spirit of Counsel
5. The Spirit of Might
6. The Spirit of Knowledge
7. The Spirit of the Fear of the Lord

Each of these seven spirits will be received by the church during the unique dynamics of the end-times. Each of these seven spirits will be received by the Church that reveals herself in seven characteristics shown in the end-times to empower her to endure to the end to her glorified and purified state as a bride adorned for her husband. These seven spirits seen in the seven golden candlesticks of the Revelation of John is what will cause the church to be a light to the Jews and the world to enlighten the way of the Lord and bring the nations to Jesus.

Isa 60:1 Arise, shine; for thy light is come, and the glory of the LORD is risen upon thee. 2 For, behold, the darkness shall cover the earth, and gross darkness the people: but the LORD shall arise upon thee, and his glory shall be seen upon thee. 3 And the Gentiles shall come to thy light, and kings to the brightness of thy rising. 4 Lift up thine eyes round about, and see: all they gather themselves together, they come to thee: thy sons shall come from far, and thy daughters shall be nursed at thy side. 5 Then thou shalt see, and flow together, and thine heart shall fear, and be enlarged; because the abundance of the sea shall be converted unto thee, the forces of the Gentiles shall come unto thee.

The end-time Church will operate in these seven Spirits, seen as lights in the seven golden candlesticks. Jesus will be in the midst of her, leading her through the valley and the shadow of death as their shepherd, His rod and staff comforting them, preparing a table before them in the presence of her enemies. Again, In order for Him to lead us in direction with His staff through the end times, He's going to have to correct us with His rod, enabling us to follow him through this valley and shadow of death. This correcting of His Church is necessary for the church to be purified and led by him in the end-times. Jesus will cleanse and purify his church through the word of admonition and correction he gave to the 7 churches in the Revelation of Jesus Christ. *He that hath an ear to hear let him hear what the Spirit says to the church.*

The Church's Power to Endure and Overcome at the End of the Age

The Book of Revelation is an "Eschatological Book of Acts" revealing the acts of the Spirit through the end-time apostles and prophets and the praying Church under Jesus' authority. Jesus will have partnership with the end-time apostles and prophets in binding and loosing the events in the Book of Revelation as He did with the apostles in the Book of Acts.

He defines the spiritual maturity necessary for the Church to release the Great Tribulation by prophetic prayer under His leadership in the way that Moses released the 10 plagues on Egypt and in the way that the apostles established the Church in Acts. These 7 prophetic messages instruct us on how to prepare to partner with Jesus in His worldwide action plan related to His Second Coming. Jesus knows best how to prepare His own Bride. These letters show us the kind of Church that Jesus is building and what His agenda is. In them, He defines love and how He relates to His people. This defines what relevance is. These letters define the truths and focus necessary to equip the Church to walk in love for Jesus. Our love is expressed as we obey His commands, heed His warnings and believe His promises (especially His 22 eternal rewards). There will be great challenges but even greater rewards. There is a dynamic continuum between what we do in the years immediately preceding Jesus' return. It is essential that we walk in full obedience and are loyal to the truth about Jesus as the necessary preparation to establish these truths beyond our life, to reach others and society.

> The weapons of our warfare are not carnal but *mighty in God* for pulling down strongholds, 5 casting down arguments and every high thing that exalts itself against the knowledge of God, bringing every thought into captivity to the obedience of Christ, 6 and *being ready to punish all disobedience* when your *obedience is fulfilled* (complete: NIV, NAS RSV). (2 Cor. 10:4-6)

Once the church develops an ear to hear and eyes to see, and receives correction and direction, she can be ushered before the throne of God, and stand before the Lord sitting on the throne. Standing on the sea of glass she will receive power and glory for strength to endure the time of tribulation, and persecution that will come to test and try her as a bride without spot, wrinkle, blemish or any such thing.

Rev 4:1 After this I looked, and, behold, a door was opened in heaven: and the first voice which I heard was as it were of a trumpet talking with me; which said, Come up hither, and I will show thee things which must be hereafter. 2. and immediately I was in the spirit: and, behold, a throne was set in heaven, and one sat on the throne. 3. and he that sat was to look upon like a jasper and a sardine stone: and there was a rainbow round about the throne, in sight like unto an emerald.

CHAPTER 3

PURITY STEP #1 - CHURCH OF EPHESUS - *Repentance from leaving our first Love - Intimacy & the Bridal Paradigm*

> **Nevertheless I have somewhat against thee, because thou hast left thy first love. 7 He that hath an ear, let him hear what the Spirit saith unto the churches;** *To him that overcomes will I give to eat of the tree of life, which is in the midst of the paradise of God. Rev 2:6*

In order for the church at the end of the age to be prepared as a bride adorned for her husband without spot or wrinkle, she must be purified from her compromise, sin and cold love. She must get a revelation of Jesus' admonitions to the 7 churches of Asia from the messages given to John on the isle of Patmos. These 7 churches and their admonitions and affirmations being applied to the church at the end of the age will give us a picture of what the church will look like when she is prepared for the coming Great and Terrible Day of the Lord. This section is dedicated to exploring these seven churches and what Jesus said to them in His revelation so that we can know at the end of the age how to position ourselves as a pure bride.

The Church of Ephesus

> *Rev 2:1 Unto the angel of the church of Ephesus write; These things says he that holds the seven stars in his right hand, who walks in the midst of the seven golden candlesticks; 2. I know thy works, and thy labour, and thy patience, and how thou canst not bear them which are evil: and thou hast*

37

> *tried them which say they are apostles, and are not,
> and hast found them liars:*

Ephesus was the capital and largest city of the Roman province of Asia Minor with a population of approximately 250,000 people and a public theatre seating 25,000. It was a financial center in being a leading seaport on the Mediterranean Sea. This seaport city was known for immorality. Ephesus was also a major center for idolatry in Asia. The central place of worship in the city was the great temple of Diana, which was one of the seven wonders of the ancient world (425 feet long, 220 feet wide, 60 feet high held up by 127 marble pillars). It combined religion and sexual immorality. The silversmith trade was prosperous because of the demand for gold, silver and bronze idols of Diana to be used as one's household deity (Acts 19:25).

This church was a revival center for Asia (Acts 19:26) being the third most prominent church in the Book of Acts after Jerusalem and Antioch. It was a lamp stand bringing light to many. Paul first came to Ephesus on his way to Jerusalem from Corinth at the end his second missionary trip in AD 52 (Acts 18:19-21). He initially preached in the synagogue for several months then left. Priscilla and Aquila stayed to train Apollos and the disciples of John the Baptist (Acts 18:24-28).

Correction for Compromise: Neglect in Cultivating Love for Jesus

4 Nevertheless I have this against you, that you have left your first love. (Rev. 2:4)

They put labor and growing their ministry reaching into all Asia before cultivating a heart of love for Jesus. The first and great commandment is to love God with all our heart. This will empower us to love people much deeper and with consistency.

Lovers always outwork workers. They became like the foolish virgins parable in Mt. 25:1-13.

You have left your first love – they left or neglected their original heart of devotion for Jesus that was seen in the great revival in which the church was started in Acts 19. Service and doctrinal purity are very important but they can never replace our love for Jesus. As we come to the last days before the coming of the Lord, God is going to restore intimacy and the Love of God back to his body. Before the Lord returns the antidote for the end-time church standing in times of intense persecution and opposition is the first and great commandment being restored to first place in the body of Christ. The first and great commandment is found in Matt 22:37 *Jesus said unto him, Thou shalt love the Lord thy God with all thy heart, and with all thy soul, and with all thy mind.* This is the first and great commandment. His body is going to Love him with all of their heart soul and mind before he returns.

In order to get to a place in the body of Christ where the first commandment is returned to first place, Pastors and ministers of the gospel are going to have to focus on leading God's people somewhere other than just an event, or a so-called move of God or a breakthrough in the spirit in our church services or even revival in the communities. We can do all of that and still not Love God in a way that causes Him to be first in our lives. We can do all that and still during times of persecution, and temptation or the threat of death, give in to the temptation to compromise and take down in our faith and thusly leave our first Love. We must focus on taking the flock somewhere in their hearts where their response to God at the heart level is at a place where their Love for God is growing to a place that during the time of persecution, tribulation, or temptation they're able to stand, having done all (beforehand to be able) to stand.

In the end time days our churches will need more than good services with power and presence. The enemy will be manifesting power and a false anointing that will deceive many. We will need more than a word that tickles our ears and moves our emotions. We will need more than a vision that draws people to our ministry assignments. We will need a biblical END-TIME CAUSE with instruction that galvanizes every believer into the mission of returning to the Love for God with all our heart, preparing for the unique dynamics of the end-times and preparing the way for the coming of the LORD. Responding to God at the heart level in unconditional Love and obedience is what leads us to more of Christ. However in our religious churches our goal has become to manufacture an outward appearance of Christ being in our midst, by a move of the spirit, or by trying to prove that we are the man of faith and power for the hour, so much so that we lose focus and never deal with our lack of a heart response to God stemming from our lack of love for him. We end up never dealing with our disobedience to him and our lack of service to him with the right motives. How we loved God in view of the first commandment is what will be measured at the Judgment seat of Christ of the believer. So why are we not focusing on leading people to grow in their Love for God?

The Love of God and the Bridal Paradigm

Rev 22:17 And the Spirit and the bride say, Come. And let him that hears say, Come

We will hear much about the ***Bridal paradigm*** as we approach the coming of the Lord and the Kingdom of God. The word paradigm means perspective or view. Thus, we refer to the "bridal perspective or view" of the kingdom of God. We see the Kingdom through the eyes of a wholehearted Bride with loyal devoted love. If we do not feel loved and in love, then we more easily compromise, lack courage and become spiritually bored. The

40

Holy Spirit for the first time in history will universally emphasize the Church's spiritual identity as Jesus' Bride. This scripture does not prophesy the Spirit and the family say "Come." Nor does it say the Spirit and the army say come, nor the Spirit and the kingdom say come, nor the body, nor the temple, neither does it say the Spirit and the priesthood say come, but only *the Spirit and the Bride.* Forever, we rejoice in the reality of our spiritual identity as God's army, family, body, temple, priesthood and kingdom, but at the end of the age the last and main identity he will emphasis and restore is our spiritual identity as His Bride.

The Bridegroom Message Is a Call to Active Intimacy with God

> *The Spirit searches all things, yes, the deep things of God...12 we have received...the Spirit...that we might know (experience) the things that have been freely given to us by God. (1 Cor. 2:10-12)*

God's invitation is for us to experience the deep things of His heart (emotions, desire, affection and thoughts about us). Thus, to enjoy *active intimacy* with Jesus that includes understanding and feeling His heart. Thus, the Bridal message is experiencing Jesus' emotions (desire, affections) for us. We must return to our bridal identity in the body of Christ as the Bride of Christ. As women are the sons of God, so men are the Bride of Christ, both describe our position of privilege before God, rather than pointing to something that is intrinsically male or female. Most Christian women do not struggle with the idea of being sons of God because they do not see it as a call to be less feminine. However, often, men struggle with being the Bride of Christ because they wrongly conclude that it is a call to become less masculine, because they do not understand it as a position of privilege that enables us to encounter His heart. Some of the greatest men of

41

God functioned in the essential reality of the bridal identity. King David was Israel's greatest warrior king, yet he was a lovesick worshipper, ravished by God's desire for him and fascinated by His beauty (Ps. 27:4). One of the central issues of David's life, as a man after God's own heart, was in being a student of God's emotions and affections. John the apostle was called the Son of Thunder and he described himself five times as the one whom Jesus loved (Jn. 13:23; 19:26; 20:2; 21:7, 20).

John the Baptist was the fiery prophet that Jesus called the "greatest man" (Mt. 11:11). He understood Jesus as the Bridegroom God (Jn. 3:29). In other words, experiencing the reality of being the Bride of Christ does not undermine one's masculinity, but rather it strengthens and establishes it. To understand Jesus as a passionate Bridegroom is to soon see ourselves as cherished Bride. Intimacy causes our hearts to be lovesick for Jesus (inflamed; enraptured; overcome by His love).

> *O daughters of Jerusalem, if you find my Beloved (Jesus)...tell Him I am lovesick! (Song 5:8)*

What Is The Bridegroom Message? (Mt. 22:2; 25:1)

Jesus the Bridegroom is filled with tender mercy – He is gentle with our weakness. We often confuse rebellion and immaturity. God is angry at rebellion, but He has a heart of tenderness towards sincere believers that seek to obey Him. He enjoys us even in our weakness.

> *He delivered me because He delighted in me. 35 Your gentleness made me great. (Ps. 18:19, 35) If You, LORD, should mark iniquities...who could stand? 4 But there is forgiveness with You, that You may be feared. (Ps. 130:3-4)*

42

Jesus the Bridegroom has a heart of gladness (happy heart) – Jesus had more gladness than any man in history (Heb. 1:9). Most of Church history has viewed God as mostly mad or mostly sad when He relates to us. However, Jesus is mostly glad when He relates to us, even in our weakness.

> *God has anointed you with the oil of gladness more than your companions. (Heb. 1:9)*

Jesus the Bridegroom has fiery affections – He has burning desire and longing.

> *As the Father loved Me, I also have loved you; abide in my love. (Jn. 15:9)*

Jesus the Bridegroom is zealous – He destroys all that hinders love and injures His Church (Zech.1:14; 8:2; Ezek. 38:18-19; Rev. 19:2; Prov. 6:34)

> *Jealousy is a husband's fury, therefore, He will not spare in the day of vengeance. (Prov. 6:34)*

Jesus the Bridegroom possesses indescribable beauty – He fascinates our hearts (Ps. 27:4).

> *One thing I have desired of the LORD...that I may dwell in the house of the LORD all the days of my life, to behold the beauty of the LORD... (Ps. 27:4)*

> *Your eyes will see the King in His beauty.... (Isa. 33:17)*

Encounters with a lovesick God will energize the Church with a spirit of prayer with courage. We cry, "Come", both upwardly to

Jesus and outwardly to people (evangelism, discipleship) differently with the Bridal paradigm. The Church will be cleansed by experiencing the cherishing heart of Jesus.

> *That He might...cleanse her...by the Word...27 present her...a glorious church...29 for no one ever hated his flesh, but nourishes and cherishes it, as the Lord does the Church. (Eph. 5:26-29)*

The 3-Fold Intercessory Cry for Jesus to Come

1. *Come NEAR US in intimacy* (individual breakthrough of my heart in God)

2. *Come TO US in revival* (regional or national breakthrough of the Spirit in revival)

3. *Come FOR US in the sky* (historical breakthrough by the Second Coming of Jesus).

The 2-fold expression of the Bride's cry for Jesus to come

1. *Worship* – "We love you, we worship you, we beckon you to come by our love."

2. *Intercession* – "We need you, we pray for you to come and release revival power.

It's a two-dimensional cry upward to God and outward to people. It's *Vertical* – an upward call to Jesus to come to us in breakthrough power (near us/to us/for us). It's *Horizontal* – an outward call to people to come to Jesus as the Bridegroom King. We call believers *(revival, discipleship)* and unbelievers *(evangelism)* to experience the Bridegroom God. Most of the Western Church today is out of sync with this purpose of God. Many things will change. What will help bring about this change? The Holy Spirit is raising up forerunners.

Forerunners are those who are one short step ahead of others in walking out and announcing what the Holy Spirit will soon emphasize universally. The Spirit anoints what He emphasizes. Jesus will only come (near us/to us/for us) in response to a praying Church, and not in a vacuum. He only comes by invitation of His covenant people. In the Father's sovereignty, He has decreed to work only in partnership with a praying Church. Ministry programs can be helpful, but must not exist at the expense of the prayer ministry, which is the primary mandate of the Church. It is important to know where we are going and how to get there. The End-Time Church will surely be victorious as we are anointed in intercession in our bridal identity.

> *"...that He might sanctify and cleanse her...by the Word, that He might present...a Glorious Church...that she should be holy..." (Eph. 5:26-27)*
> *"A great multitude...of all nations...and tongues...before the Lamb" (Rev. 7:9)*
>
> *"Let us be glad...for the marriage of the Lamb has come, His wife has made herself READY....arrayed in fine linen, clean and bright..." (Rev. 19: 7-8)*

Prayer of Repentance for Leaving Our First Love

The Church of Ephesus – **Jesus We repent for leaving our first love** (*An intimate relationship with Jesus Christ*) We will return to intimacy with you, loving you with all our heart, mind, soul and strength, spending time with you as our first defense against the temptation to work or serve for your acceptance, and against the temptation of the lust of the flesh, the lust of the eyes, and the pride of life. Lord, we turn back to seeking your face. we turn to studying the bridal paradigm of your heart and emotions of love for us as your bride, found in the Song of Solomon. We covenant to keep a sacred charge for personal and corporate prayer times in prayer room gatherings in your body, to intercede for your church to return the first commandment to Love you with all our heart, mind, soul and strength, to first place in our midst.

CHAPTER 4

PURITY STEP #2 - CHURCH OF SMYRNA -
Repentance from fear of suffering tribulation-becoming faithful unto death

> *Rev 2:8 And unto the angel of the church in Smyrna write; These things saith the first and the last, which was dead, and is alive; 9 I know thy works, and tribulation, and poverty, (but thou art rich) and I know the blasphemy of them which say they are Jews, and are not, but are the synagogue of Satan. 10* **Fear none of those things which thou shalt suffer: behold, the devil shall cast some of you into prison, that ye may be tried; and ye shall have tribulation ten days: be thou faithful unto death**, *and I will give thee a crown of life. 11* <u>**He that hath an ear, let him hear what the Spirit saith unto the churches;**</u>

The second step to the purifying of end-time Church is repentance from the fear of suffering tribulation in order to become faithful unto death. When we are purified from the fear of suffering tribulation and become faithful unto death, as the church of Smyrna, we will become a House of Prayer again, praying day & night prayers for justice on our adversary as is recorded in Luke 18:7 of the widow woman pleading for justice from the unjust judge. In the church in the West we have adopted a comfort, prosperity, blessing gospel that calls anything that involves any type of suffering or persecution ungodly. We feel it is an indication of something gone wrong with our faith in God, or with our walk with God. However, Jesus warned the church of Smyrna to fear none of the things which they would suffer. He told them that they would suffer tribulation, but to be faithful unto death in order that they may receive a crown of life. At the end of the age the prayers of the martyred saints are what's going to loose the judgments of the bowls, and trumpets on the Anti-Christ system as depicted in the book of the revelation of Jesus Christ.

> *Rev 6:9 And when he had opened the fifth seal, I saw under the altar the souls of them that were slain for the word of God, and for the testimony which they held: 10 And they cried with a loud voice, saying, How long, O Lord, holy and true, dost thou not judge and avenge our blood on them that dwell on the earth? 11 And white robes were given unto every one of them; and it was said unto them, that they should rest yet for a little season, until their fellow servants also and their brethren, that should be killed as they were, should be fulfilled.*

Just as instances of miraculous deliverance, provision, protection, and healing are part of the normal Christian life in this age, so also is suffering of various kinds and degrees. And just as the LORD has a design to magnify Jesus in displaying His miraculous power, He also has a design to magnify Jesus in restraining His power. The glory of God is in the face of Christ as exalted King *and* Suffering Servant.

The common idea that obedience and faithfulness to Jesus in this age will result in a consistent ascent of comfort in domestic affairs, peace in relationships, and popularity or favorable recognition in ministry is foreign to the New Testament. The question is not if we will suffer, but rather *when and how*. Having this delusion shattered is necessary if we are to glorify Christ in the midst of it and if our hearts are to persevere through it at the end of the age. To persist in error related to God's leadership and suffering will leave one either offended with God (for not fulfilling

48

His supposed obligation to procure our comfort) or condemning themselves (for the supposed sin or unbelief that has caused it). ... *36 Still others had trial of mockings and scourgings, yes, and of chains and imprisonment. 37 They were stoned, they were sawn in two, were tempted, were slain with the sword. They wandered about in sheepskins and goatskins, being destitute, afflicted, tormented — 38 of whom the world was not worthy. They wandered in deserts and mountains, in dens and caves of the earth. 39 And all these, having obtained a good testimony through faith... Hebrew 11:36-40*

All hardship we face comes with the promise that the tender compassion of Jesus is with us *in it*, the assurance of the ultimate eradication *of it*, and the confidence that God has a design *for it –* a design for *His glory* and for *our good*. We want to avoid suffering at all cost, using whatever resources we have to stay immune from its reach – even at the expense of others. And when our options are depleted and we finally must succumb to it, our response typically borders on the total opposite of the Bible. If our plans are disrupted, if we are unrecognized, overlooked or mistreated, if we are inconvenienced and our aspirations thwarted by the needs of others, if we experience sickness or pain, if our comfort is stripped from us, and if we are suddenly hemmed in by limitation, our primary reaction is *anger*. It may be the quiet anger of resentment, the cold anger of hard-heartedness, the conniving anger of manipulation, or the burning anger of rage, *but it is not joy*. If this is the case of those who sincerely love Jesus, *what will be the lot of the unregenerate man?*

Magnifying Jesus & God's Design

The contrast between the biblical reaction to suffering and that which is common to man, explains why pain and persecution is such fertile ground for magnifying Christ. Two primary (not only) ways that we magnify Jesus in this age while He is not with us are:

1) by rejoicing in Him in the midst of suffering; and 2) by mourning for Him in the midst of ease. These two acts both expose the *worthlessness* of what has captured the devotion of humanity and the exceeding *worthiness* of Jesus to capture the devotion of humanity. When we shed tears of joy in the midst of sickness, or beatings, or mistreatment, or pain of any kind, it reveals that whatever was lost through those things does not compare to the beauty of who Jesus is – a treasure which we possess and can never lose.

The Primary Message of the Church of Smyrna

The church of Smyrna was a persecuted church. Jesus called them to fearlessness and faithfulness that would require some of them to die for their faith. He honored them for their enduring persecution and financial poverty. He told them that more persecution was coming but promised them the crown of life.

The City Of Smyrna

Smyrna was a large harbor city on the Aegean Sea (west coast of modern Turkey) with over 100,000 residents. It continues today as the city of Izmir with a population of about 200,000. This heavily persecuted city is the only city of the seven mentioned in Rev. 2-3, that still exists today. Satan could not stamp out their testimony. It was one of the most beautiful cities in Asia being referred to in the ancient world as "the Crown of Asia" or "the Flower of Asia. It was a prosperous harbor with many roads connecting it to the major cities of Asia. All were required by law to worship at a pagan temple. The most prominent were the temples to Zeus and the goddess Cybele. Emperor worship was a unifying factor in the Roman Empire.

Once a year, all were required to burn incense on an altar for Caesar. Christians who refused to participate in this were considered criminals of the state. They were burned at the stake or killed by wild beasts. There was a large influential Jewish population who persecuted the church.

Jesus' Revelation of Himself

> *8 These things says the First and the Last, who was dead, and came to life... (Rev. 2:8)*

The First and the Last – refers back to Rev. 1:17-18 and is mentioned seven times (Isa. 41:4; 44:6; 48:12; Rev. 1:8, 17; 2:8; 22:13). In Isaiah (3x) and Revelation (4x). He is the "First" source of all blessing and is the "Last" to stand. This assures us that all His promises will come to pass. The beginning and end of His plan for our life are in His loving powerful hands.

Jesus was dead, and came to life – to a church with martyrs, Jesus revealed Himself as a man who died but conquered death. Jesus as the eternal God who was "First" became a man who embraced the pain of death and as one with the power over it. He experienced the worst that men can do to us and triumphed over it. Jesus understands what His people go through.

Perfect Love to Cast out Fear in the Day of Judgment

> *1Jn 4:17,18 Herein is our love made perfect, that we may have boldness in the day of judgment: because as he is, so are we in this world. There is no fear in love; but perfect love casts out fear: because fear hath torment. He that fears is not made perfect in love.*

> *The word PERFECT-Mteleioō, tel-i-o'-o; to complete,*

51

> *that is, (literally) accomplish, or (figuratively) consummate (in character): - consecrate, finish, fulfill, (make) perfect; complete (in various applications of labor, growth, mental and moral character, etc.); completeness: - of full age, man, perfect.*

Our love is made complete, consummate in character, complete in growth, mental and moral character, full aged, grown, matured through suffering in the day of the great and terrible day of the Lord. In that day our love is made complete, matured in growth, and full aged, by continuing to dwell in God and God in us in the midst of suffering. We will dwell in God and God in us when we believe and know the love that God has toward us even in the midst of persecution. This is what God reveals to us in the place of day and night prayer. It's a season of God showing us how much he loves us so that when the suffering comes as a purifying agent of the Love of God we won't be fearful or be offended. That's what this end-time prayer movement is going to produce. It's going to prepare us to have boldness in the Day of Judgment, that as Christ suffered so will we in the world.

> *John 15:20,21 Remember the word that I said unto you, The servant is not greater than his lord. If they have persecuted me, they will also persecute you; if they have kept my saying, they will keep yours also. But all these things will they do unto you for my name's sake, because they know not him that sent me.*

When we know and believe the love that God hath to us we will dwell in God's love and therein have our love made perfect, and this will give us boldness in the Day of Judgment.

> *1Jn 4:16 And we have known and believed the love*
> *that God hath to us. God is love; and he that dwells*
> *in love dwells in God, and God in him.*

I believe this verse is saying that as we dwell or continue in him through persecution and suffering our love will mature to the point that our knowing and believing that he loves us will empower us so that not only will we have boldness in the Day of Judgment, but we would be willing die for him. This type of love, a sacrificial love overcomes the fear of dying. It makes dying a cinch. We have boldness in the face of death, sickness, disease, loss, tragedy. There's no fear.   Because there is no fear in love; but perfect, mature, grown love casts out all fear. Therefore we must grow in love because there will come a day of judgment for our love. And when that day of judgment comes there must be no fear. We will have no fear, but boldness, willing to lay down our lives for him. He that fears has not had his love matured. His love has not grown to the point that he could boldly look the judgment of death in the face and not fear but go calmly and resolutely to that fate.

Repenting from the fear of suffering Persecution in the 21st Century Church

1Jn 4:19 we love him, because he first loved us.

I believe this is saying that we are willing to show our love by dying for him because he first showed his love for us by dying for us. The First century saints understood this. This was always in the front of their minds when they faced persecution and death. He said this would happen. It happened to him and so we have been prepared for this hour.   They were ready to stand for Jesus, knowing all he did for them. The church of the 21st century must repent and be purified from this fear of persecution and death which has caused us to gravitate to a gospel that was not seen, heard or preached in the first century church. The reason we have a pre-tribulation rapture mentality when it comes to the judgment that shall begin at the house of God is because we have a worldly unbiblical view of suffering and dying. We think that suffering is God's disapproval of us. We think that suffering must be an indication that he's mad at us, that it's God's wrath. But it's actually unwarranted, undeserved suffering that is our greatest opportunity to show the Love of God. It's our greatest opportunity to show him that our love for him has matured to its highest extent.

> *1Pe 2:19 for this is thankworthy, if a man for conscience toward God endure grief, suffering wrongfully. 20 for what glory is it, if, when ye be buffeted for your faults, ye shall take it patiently? but if, when ye do well, and suffer for it, ye take it patiently, this is acceptable with God. 21 for even hereunto were ye called: because Christ also suffered for us, leaving us an example, that ye should follow his steps:*

Jesus taught his disciples again and again that His purpose for coming was not comfort and ease but Death. As a matter of fact, I believe Jesus hesitated on telling anyone who he really was because he knew they would be confused when he fulfilled the actual purpose for why he came in his first incarnation – DEATH.

> *Mat 16:20 Then charged he his disciples that they should tell no man that he was Jesus the Christ. 21 From that time forth began Jesus to shew unto his disciples, how that he must go unto Jerusalem, and suffer many things of the elders and chief priests and scribes, and be killed, and be raised again the third day.*

Why did Jesus tell them that they should not tell anyone who he was? The answer is found in the text. Because his purpose was to go to Jerusalem suffer many things of the elders and chief priests and scribes and die. His purpose in His first coming was not to overthrow Rome. I believe he knew that if they knew he was the Messiah, they would immediately try to make him king and begin preparing for the overthrow of Rome, keeping him from his purpose, which was the cross. He begins to explain to them His purpose in verse 21, that he was going to Jerusalem and that he would suffer many things and be killed and be raised again the third day from the dead. And what does Peter do?

> *Mat 16:22 Then Peter took him, and began to rebuke him, saying, Be it far from thee, Lord: this shall not be unto thee.*

He responds the way that anyone would that just got a revelation of who Jesus really was – *The Christ*. That's why I believe he told them not to tell anyone who he was, because he knew the people would respond the same way Peter responded once he knew who he was.

> *Mat 16:23 But he turned, and said unto Peter, Get thee behind me, Satan: thou art an offence unto me: for thou savourest not the things that be of God, but those that be of men.*

What does Jesus do? He rebukes Satan, and let's Peter know; you're trying to stop my purpose of coming to the earth. You're an offense to me. You're my enemy right now. We can readily see as a result of looking at these verses that Jesus was struggling with telling the disciples who he was because they would not understand his purpose of dying on the cross.

A Cross has been Passed onto Us

It should be clear now that Jesus was getting them ready for his destiny in the Cross. However, rarely do we connect the next verses with the previous text, where he talks to them about his followers experiencing the same fate as him.

> *Mat 16:24 Then said Jesus unto his disciples, If any man will come after me, let him deny himself, and take up his cross, and follow me. 25 For whosoever will save his life shall lose it: and whosoever will lose his life for my sake shall find it. 26 For what is a man profited, if he shall gain the whole world, and lose his own soul? or what shall a man give in exchange for his soul?*

We often preach this verse to be a symbolic death of denying what we want and what we desire in this life. But Jesus was telling them, "Look, not only am I going to be killed for this cause, but most of you standing here are going to die the same why I'm about to die in the next few weeks.

> *Mat 16:27 For the Son of man shall come in the glory of his Father with his angels; and then he shall reward every man according to his works. 28 Verily I say unto you, there be some standing here, which shall not taste of death, till they see the Son of man coming in his kingdom.*

Jesus was telling them, if you really follow me there's a good chance you will die a violent death on your own type of cross just as I'm about to. He tells them, "Some of you (one) standing here will not taste death, (through martyrdom) till they see the son of man coming in his kingdom." I believe he was speaking of John, who would not die a martyr's death. He would die of old age.

John was the only one standing there that did not die a martyr's death. John did not die until he saw the glorified Christ coming in his kingdom on the isles of Patmos.

Jesus was showing them how they were supposed to look at death and how they was supposed to face their own death – embrace it, settle it now, accept it. It's what's going to cause you to see my kingdom come and my will be done in earth as it is in heaven. But because we think unwarranted suffering, persecution and death is something negative to be withstood and resisted, many in the body of Christ justify not going through the Great tribulation because some will end up dying a martyr's death to see Justice released on the Anti-Christ and his system in the earth. Unwarranted suffering is always redemptive. And it always releases God's swift judgment in the earth (Luke 18:7, 8). Much of the body of Christ has used scripture that has been twisted to justify the pre-tribulation rapture, quoting scriptures like, *"God has not given us to wrath."*

Though he has not given us to wrath, this does not mean God has not given us to suffering, and death. The book of Hebrews says it's appointed unto men once to die. We, in the church, mistakenly associate unwarranted suffering unto death with God's wrath and Judgment. And though God's wrath will be released on all ungodliness, on the believer God's judgment is all about removing everything within and around us that hinders love. His Judgment will be released to purify love and bring a demarcation between those who are truly God's and those who are not. Those who are truly God's will stand in the face of persecution and opposition, being faithful unto death. Suffering and death are a part of the life of the believer. Being a believer doesn't exempt you from suffering or death. No more than Jesus, being the son of God, was exempted from suffering and death.

We're all going to suffer some time in our life and we're all going to die. But as a believer we don't suffer or die because we've sinned but because we Love God with all our heart, mind, soul and strength. And God's love is not love without a sacrifice. Suffering and a willingness to sacrifice and lay down your life for another actually purifies and proves our love for God and one another. When we are purified from the fear of suffering and are faithful unto death, as the church of Smyrna, we will become a House of Prayer again praying day & night prayers for Jesus to return to avenge us of our adversary.

> *Luk 18:6 And the Lord said, Hear what the unjust judge saith. 7 And shall not God avenge his own elect, which cry day and night unto him, though he bear long with them? 8 I tell you that he will avenge them speedily. Nevertheless when the Son of man cometh, shall he find faith on the earth?*

Prayer of Repentance from fear of suffering Tribulation

The Church of Smyrna - **We repent for the fear of suffering tribulation** and turn to the faithfulness of Christ unto death. (Matt 16:20). Lord, we turn to living and studying to have a mind that is girt with the sufferings of Christ, desiring the fellowship of Christ's sufferings, over the 21st century gospel of comfort and convenience. (1 Peter 4:1-12)

CHAPTER 5

PURITY STEP # 3 - CHURCH OF PERGAMOS
Repentance from the false doctrine of Balaam-fornication in the Church

*Rev 2:12 And to the angel of the church in Pergamos write; These things saith he; 13 I know thy works, and where thou dwellest, even where Satan's seat is: and thou holdest fast my name, and hast not denied my faith, even in those days wherein Antipas was my faithful martyr, who was slain among you, where Satan dwelleth. 14 But I have a few things against thee, because thou hast there them that hold the doctrine of Balaam, who taught Balac to cast a stumblingblock before the children of Israel, **to eat things sacrificed unto idols, and to commit fornication.** 16 **Repent; or else I will come unto thee quickly, and will fight against them with the sword of my mouth. 17 He that hath an ear, let him hear what the Spirit saith unto the churches;**

The Church of Pergamos was a church that held fast his name, and had many faithful martyrs like Antipas, however, Jesus lets us know through His admonition to this church that faithfulness unto death is not enough if you are not revealing your love also through allowing Him to purify us of doctrines that seem to permit fornication and eating any and everything we want when we want it.   Pergamos was encouraged for their faithfulness as they were called to stand up against false teaching that tolerated compromise with idolatrous feasts which were like "parties filled with immorality."

59

The Church Of Pergamos

The Church in Pergamos was in a wealthy city and that was a center for idol worship. It was about 20 miles from the Aegean Sea. It is also spelled Pergamum, Pergamus or Pergamon, It had a large university with a famous library of 200,000 volumes. Today, the village of Bergama is on the ancient site. It was the first city in Asia to build a temple to worship the Emperor. In 29 BC, the temple for Augustus was completed making it the religious capital in the east as Rome was in the west. The throne of Satan refers to a multitude of major altars of worship to the four most prominent Greek gods: Zeus, Athena, Dionysos, and Asclepius (Esculapius) along with being the center of Emperor worship for Asia. Each had a priesthood with temple prostitution. When the cult of the Magians was driven out of Babylon, it was relocated to Pergamos.

Jesus' Revelation of Himself

> *12 These things says He who has the sharp two-edged sword... (Rev. 2:12)*

The sword comes from Jesus' mouth to release judgment on His enemies (Rev. 1:16; 19:15, 21).

> *15 Out of His mouth goes a sharp sword, that with it He should strike nations... 21 The rest were killed with the sword which proceeded from the mouth of Him... (Rev. 19:15, 21)*

Jesus uses the sword of His mouth to withstand the threats of evil governments such as ancient Rome and especially the Antichrist government at the end-of-the-age. He uses the sword of His mouth to war against sin and darkness anywhere that it is persisted in.

Affirmation for Faithfulness

> *13 I know your works, and where you dwell, where Satan's throne is. And you hold fast to My name, and did not deny My faith even in the days in which Antipas was My faithful martyr, who was killed among you, where Satan dwells. (Rev. 2:13)*

I know you dwell where Satan's throne is and where Satan dwells – in Pergamos there was reference to a complex of pagan temples and demonic activity.

As Rome was the center of Satan's activity in the West so Pergamos was his "throne" in the East. Satan's throne or center of manifest power and activity is also in other cities. Will the throne of the Antichrist in Rev. 16:10 be at Pergamos?

Satan's activities will escalate in the Tribulation to fill the earth with Satan worship, etc. *21 They did not repent of their murders...sorceries or their sexual immorality... (Rev. 9:21)*

I know your works – Jesus understood the dynamics in which they had to minister. **You hold fast to My name, and did not deny My faith** – Jesus knew that many held fast to His name in the midst of so much satanic activity. To hold fast to Jesus' name refers to doctrinal purity and faithfulness even in the face of death. Jesus will give us power to be faithful in the midst of hostile and sinful cultures. We hold fast to Jesus' name in the End-times by refusing the mark of the Beast (Rev. 13:13-17). We will do this by using the authority of God's Word by speaking it with our mouths.

> *11They overcame him by the blood of the Lamb and by the word of their testimony, and they did not love their lives to the death. (Rev. 12:11)*

Antipas was My faithful martyr – tradition says that Antipas was the bishop in Pergamos and that he was placed in a copper vessel which was heated by fire and boiled to death. Jesus is called the faithful witness (Rev 1:5). He referred to Antipas with this title. Jesus will have a multitude of faithful witnesses who will be with Him as He makes war with Antichrist to end the Armageddon Campaign.

Correction for Compromise

> *14 But I have a few things against you, because you have there those who hold the doctrine of Balaam, who taught Balak to put a stumbling block before the children of Israel, to eat things sacrificed to idols, and to commit sexual immorality. 15 Thus you also have those who hold the doctrine of the Nicolaitans, which thing I hate. (Rev. 2:14-15)*

I have a few things against you – the two groups (Balaamites and Nicolaitans) were similar yet distinct. They both taught a perversion of the doctrine of liberty. They taught that it was okay to participate in the "partying and immorality" of that day under the pretense of Christian liberty.

> *4 Certain men have crept in unnoticed, who long ago were marked out for this condemnation, ungodly men, who turn the grace of our God into lewdness... (Jude 4)*

Antinomianism is the belief that the Gospel frees us from obedience to specific moral standards since we believe that salvation is given as a gift by faith, therefore, we do not need to repent. [Greek: *anti-nomos* (law)].**You have there those who hold the doctrine of Balaam** – the doctrine of Balaam involved participating in temple feasts and their orgies. Some of the leaders in the church taught it was okay to participate in these parties or pagan feasts.

Who taught Balak to put a stumbling block before Israel, to eat things sacrificed to idols, and to commit sexual immorality – Balaam advised King Balak to defeat the Israelites by getting them to participate in feasts related to idolatry and immorality (Num. 25). This caused God to judge Israel. The Israelites came under God's judgment as 24,000 people died.

A stumbling block is a trap that when triggered, shuts on its prey. This refers to anything which causes a person to fall into sin. ***You also have those who hold the doctrine of the Nicolaitans, which thing I hate –*** this refers to followers of Nicolas, the Jerusalem deacon who fell into error (Acts 6:5). This was the common view among the early church Fathers. For example, Irenaeus in the second century taught that the Nicolaitans were without restraint in their indulgence of the flesh, especially with immorality. This distortion of "liberty in grace" that allows for compromise with a sinful culture is prevalent in the church today. This view best represents what Jesus was saying in this passage. This doctrine and practice was also prominent in Ephesus (Rev. 2:6).

> *6 But this you have, that you hate the deeds of the Nicolaitans, which I also hate. (Rev. 2:6)*

Twice Jesus mentions His hatred of the Nicolaitans. What were ***deeds*** in Ephesus were ***doctrines*** in Pergamos. The teaching allowed the spirit of compromise to go unchallenged. The church continued to allow those who held the teaching of Balaam and the Nicolaitans. They had not purged themselves of such as the church in Ephesus did (Rev. 2:6).

Exhortation to Respond (With a Warning)

> *16 Repent, or else I will come to you quickly and will fight against them with the sword of My mouth. (Rev. 2:16)*

Repent – we must turn away from personal compromise and tolerance of it in the Church. *I will come to you quickly* – Jesus comes to His Church to evaluate it at specific seasons.

> *3 If you will not watch, I will come upon you as a thief, and you will not know what hour I will come upon you. (Rev. 3:3)*

I will fight against them with the sword of My mouth – Jesus will release the sword of His mouth in judgment against this toleration in the church. Jesus will cleanse His Church. This is not a reference to the Second Coming but a coming related to this church's failure to repent.

The Stand of Phinehas against the Doctrine of Balaam

If the end-time House of Prayer for all Nations ever going to overcome the spirit of Balaam - *fornication* in the Church, it's going to require that this generation understand and take the purity stand of Phinehas. Phinehas was the Son of Eleazar, the high priest (Exo 6:25) of Israel, and he first comes on this scene in biblical history in Numbers. Phinehas was born from the marriage of Eleazar the son of Aaron to the daughters of Putiel. While yet a youth Phinehas distinguished himself at Shittim by his zeal against the immorality into which the Moabites had tempted the people (Num 25:1-9), and thus "stayed the plague" that had broken out among the people, and by which twenty-four thousand of them perished.

> *11 Phinehas...has turned back My wrath from the children of Israel, because he was zealous with My zeal among them, so that I did not consume the children of Israel in My zeal. 12 Therefore say, "Behold, I give to him My covenant of peace; 13 and it shall be to him and his descendants after him a covenant of an everlasting priesthood, because he was zealous for his God, and made atonement for the children of Israel." (Num 25:11-12)*

Phinehas filled with God's zeal stood up against the sin that Balaam helped facilitate. Balaam was eventually killed by the sword (Num. 22:23, 31; 25:5; 31:8). However, the Lord sent an angel to warn Balaam with a drawn sword to obey God's Word. He would have been killed with the sword earlier if it had not been for his donkey speaking up (Num. 22:22-25). Phinehas was raised up as a young man that was not influenced by this climate and false message of grace within the camp of Israel to take a stand against the message and the resulting acts of immorality within the camp. In Numbers 25 he was said to be zealous for His God and rose up from among the congregation and took his javelin in his hand and thrust them both the man from Israel and the Midianitish woman through their belly.

> *Num 25:6 And, behold, one of the children of Israel came and brought unto his brethren a Midianitish woman in the sight of Moses, and in the sight of all the congregation of the children of Israel, who were weeping before the door of the tabernacle of the congregation. 7 And when Phinehas, the son of Eleazar, the son of Aaron the priest, saw it, he rose up from among the congregation, and took a javelin in his hand; 8. And he went after the man of Israel into the tent, and thrust both of them through, the man of Israel, and the woman through*

65

her belly. So the plague was stayed from the children of Israel.

The Javelin through the Belly of Compromise Purifies Sexual Impurity

God is looking for young men that will rise up and be zealous for God, not being influenced by the climate of the false identity of stereo-typical sexuality in a gender or race, nor by the false grace message in the church of this generation, taking their javelin in their hand and thrusting it through the belly of the body of Christ that is compromising with immorality. Why did Phinehas drive the javelin through the belly? Why not the heart? Why not the temples in the head like Jael, Heber's wife did when she took a nail of the tent and drove it through the temples of Sisera in Judges 4:21? What does the belly represent? The Belly is the part of the body where life flows from. It's the part of the body where new life is birthed from. John 7:37, 38 says of the belly, that it releases living water from the body of Christ. This not only represents words of life spoken from the word of God, but it also represents the intimacy of relations that results in the semen being released from a man to a woman to produce life.

> *John 7:37 In the last day, that great day of the feast, Jesus stood and cried, saying, If any man thirst, let him come unto me, and drink. 38 He that believeth on me, as the scripture hath said, <u>out of his belly shall flow rivers of living water</u>. 39 (But this spake he of the Spirit, which they that believe on him should receive: for the Holy Ghost was not yet given; because that Jesus was not yet glorified.)*

The javelin through the belly of the compromising body of Christ signifies the stopping of the plague of sin and its consequences of lack of true intimacy, barrenness, poverty, sickness and spiritual death that will be stayed by the end-time Phinehas generation that will be raised up to initiate true intimacy and an everlasting priesthood, and covenant of peace to the end-time generation.

> *Num 25:12.13 Wherefore say, Behold, I give unto him my covenant of peace: 13 And he shall have it, and his seed after him, even the covenant of an everlasting priesthood; because he was zealous for his God, and made an atonement for the children of Israel.*

What is this covenant of peace that flows from and is synonymous with this everlasting priesthood of Phinehas? The covenant of peace that will be released to establish this everlasting priesthood with the body of Christ will consist of SHALOM – *Nothing missing, Nothing Broken.* God wants to give this generation the zealousness of Phinehas that turns His wrath away from the people of God.

Promise for Overcomers

> *17 He who has an ear, let him hear what the Spirit says to the churches. To him who overcomes I will give some of the hidden manna to eat. And I will give him a white stone, and on the stone a new name written which no one knows except him who receives it. (Rev. 2:17-17)*

I will give some of the hidden manna to eat – it was hidden only after it was put in the golden pot in the Ark of the Covenant in the Holy of Holies (Ex. 16:32-36; Heb. 9:1-5). This speaks of having increased capacity to be fed by the revelation of the Word in this age and in the age-to come. Hidden manna suggests the Marriage Supper of the Lamb. Only the high priest could see this hidden manna once a year, on the Day of Atonement, as he entered the Holy of Holies.

Jesus is the true bread or manna from heaven that sustains us (Jn 6:48-51). The over-comer is promised full enjoyment of something he already has a foretaste of. God supernaturally sustained His people in the OT with manna. The manna was called angel's food' (Psa.78:19-25). In the Tribulation, God's people will receive natural manna' in the wilderness (Rev. 12:6, 14).

Prayer of Repentance for Allowing the Doctrine of Balaam (Fornication) in the Church

***The Church of Pergamos* - We repent for allowing the false doctrine of Balaam - (fornication in the church),** *which is the toleration of fornication through the teaching of the Nicoliatans which taught a perversion of the doctrine of liberty. We repent of Antinomianism, which is the belief that the gospel frees us from obedience to specific moral standards since we believe that Salvation is a gift by faith through grace. Therefore we don't need to repent. <u>Lord, we turn from the spirit and eyes of adultery and fornication and commit not talk to other women on the phone, texting or on Facebook unless our wives or husbands are aware of it</u>.*

CHAPTER 6

PURITY STEP #4 - CHURCH OF THYATIRA
Repentance for allowing the Spirit of Jezebel to operate in the House

Rev 2:18 And unto the angel of the church in Thyatira write;These things saith the Son of God, who hath his eyes like unto a flame of fire, and his feet are like fine brass; 19 I know thy works, and charity, and service, and faith, and thy patience, and thy works; and the last to be more than the first. 20 **<u>Notwithstanding I have a few things against thee, because thou sufferest that woman Jezebel, which calleth herself a prophetess, to teach and to seduce my servants to commit fornication, and to eat things sacrificed unto idols.</u>** *21 And I gave her space to repent of her fornication; and she repented not. 22 Behold, I will cast her into a bed, and them that commit adultery with her into great tribulation, except they repent of their deeds. 29* **He that hath an ear, let him hear what the Spirit saith unto the churches.**

The Church of Thyatira

Thyatira was a wealthy city because it had the trade guilds which were like the ancient version of the labor unions, called trade guilds. The people involved in these labor unions were required to attend the feast, which gave thanks to the false god Apollo, for their prosperity. Everybody had to do it. It was social, but there was a lot of pressure. Some of them really believed it mattered. In these idolatrous feasts, there was much immorality and drunkenness. Many people in the ancient world, in the body of Christ, had a lot of pressure put on them, even by members in the body of Christ, saying, "It is OK to do that. The Lord understands. You have to keep your job. Go there, but do not partake of that spirit."

That is what Jezebel was teaching them. Not that they could just go to those events, but that they could participate in them because it did not really defile their spirit anyway. They still felt the presence of God. They would say, "I still feel the grace of God, so I engaged in a little drunkenness and immorality. It is not that big of a deal." Jesus said, "This I have against you: you tolerate that mindset."

Revelation 2:18:"These things says the Son of Man who has eyes like a flame of fire and His feet like fine brass." What are the eyes of fire? Fire speaks of love and holiness because love and holiness are identical. We can call it holy love. Every movement in our heart toward holiness is love. Every movement in our heart toward love is holiness. There is no such thing as something that is tender in love, but it is unholy. If it is true love, it is holy, and if it is true holiness, it is love. Jesus says, "My eyes are a fire" (v. 18, paraphrased). It's as if He says, "I will look upon you, and if you open your heart to Me, I will impart fire to help you resist the fire of immorality. But if you do not receive the fire of My help, I will look with the same eyes, and there will be a fire of judgment to wake you up." It is a fire of grace that awakens our heart in love, and we go from glory to glory, or it is a fire of judgment. It is not angry judgment. It actually is judgment because God is so committed to His relationship with us. He will not let us go uncontested with that which is destroying our spirit. He is so jealous.

The primary message of the church of Thyatira was that Jesus is affirming them for their increased outreach ministries. He says, "The works that you did are even increasing." He makes that point and then He says, "You even have love." (v. 19, paraphrased). He never told any of the churches they had love. He never told a church that they had works —ministry—and love. The Ephesians had a lot of works. That was good, it meant service. Service is good, but not if it causes our love to be diminished and waning. Here He says, "You have service and love, and you have perseverance—or endurance—in difficulty." (v. 19, paraphrased).

This was an awesome church, but the thing they lacked was not that the majority of them were involved in immorality, it was that the leadership and the people as well, did not resist it and openly oppose it. They tolerated the presence of immorality and teachers who were promoting it. The Lord says, "I know you love me, but this is not OK with me. Your silence is not OK with me." I would go as far as saying that the vast majority of the church in the western world, I would hate to say ninety percent but it is probably true, would be guilty of this lack. The unwillingness to lift their voice against this ever-increasing demonic invasion into the church called immorality. It is coming right into the homes at such a rapid speed through this thing called pornography.

The Spirit of Jezebel

The essence of the spirit of Jezebel is the spirit of immorality. A lot of people think about Jezebel and think of a woman with a strong personality. If her leadership is stronger than yours and you are a man, she is a Jezebel. But the core meaning of a Jezebel spirit is a spirit of seduction. The people most engaged in the spirit of Jezebel are men. They are the ones who are producing it, they are promoting it, they are partaking of it even more than women are. The most powerful Jezebel institution in the earth is Hollywood, California—the spirit of Jezebel, pumping volumes of filth into the nations of the earth. There must be a couple of other centers like that. If it is not number one, it is way up there. So again, when you think Jezebel, do not think of a woman with a strong personality. Maybe she needs a little bit of relationship skills to go with it and she just needs a little help on this and that. I care about that a lot because I have watched over the years, a lot of woman getting written off as a Jezebel spirit because their personality is strong. Again, they just need to get a few rough edges as well as their personality skills refined. A lot of guys have the same problem and nobody says "Jezebel" to them. We are missing the whole thing because this is not the essence of what the spirit of Jezebel even is.

The Church in America

The spirit of Jezebel is alive and well in the church in America. Again, the group that is most responsible for Jezebel is mostly men. Men are the ones that are financing the pornography industry and the whole industry of immorality. It is being financed by men, promoted by men, and is partaken of by men. And women are involved in it as well, obviously. I want us to get a real grip on what Jesus is saying so that we do not marginalize the weightiness and seriousness of what He is saying to the church. I look at the church in America and I just have one huge statement about it. There is a Jezebel spirit from coast to coast, all through the church. It is a spirit of toleration of immorality. That is bad, but the warnings that Jesus gives the spirit of Jezebel are really serious. He says to the church that has this spirit on them, which is to me, the vast majority of the body of Christ in the western world. He says, "I will send judgment to you and I will wake you up because I love you that much."

Correction for Compromise

Verse 20: "Nevertheless I have a few things against you, because you allow that woman Jezebel who calls herself a prophetess, to teach and seduce my servants to commit sexual immorality and to eat things sacrificed to idols." Verse 24(paraphrased): "I say to you and to the rest in Thyatira, as many as do not have this doctrine, who have not known the depths of Satan, I will put on you no other burden."
He goes on and gives a message to them.

Verse 20: "A few things I have against you." It is important to know that Jesus gives one of the strongest affirmations—a five-fold affirmation—to this church, but He still has things that trouble His heart against that church. As long as Jesus is still talking to us, we have a hope and a good future. His correction is not rejection. He is talking, He is talking through His Word. That is how it starts. He speaks to our conscience. It's as if the Lord says, "Do it my way. Do it my way." We say, "OK." But we do not follow through. He says, "Do it my way. I tell you, if my Word will discipline your conscience, it is done and it is finished."

"I am trying to, but I do not want to." He says, "OK, I will allow some frustrations to happen to get your attention." So the frustrations mount up. Not that all frustrations are in this category. I do not want to join Job's friendship group, his home group, those three guys who thought everything Job did was related to sin— I do not want to be in that home group. They thought everybody's trouble was related to their sin. That is not true at all. There are many troubles that are just the direct attack of the devil. However, the Lord will allow frustrations to get our attention because of continued compromise. Then the guy says, "No, I am going to keep going." The Lord says, "OK, now I am going to really get your attention. I am going to expose you openly." The thing is building to more than a frustration. They keep going. It's as if the Lord says, "OK, I am going to allow your body to be touched in a way that is really going to get your attention because I do not want to talk to you this way, when we stand face to face in eternity. Then you would really be in trouble. I will take you at any level that you will agree. We will end the trouble there."

The force and the weightiness with which Jesus speaks to us increases in its weightiness season by season. As long as He is talking to us, we have a hope of a great future. It is when He does not talk anymore, that we are in big trouble. He says, "OK, you know what, you just stay in that affair. You just stay there." One, two, three, four years and you have not felt the conviction of the Holy Spirit. That is really troubling. You are in the final stages of trouble.   However, if you are wrestling, you are sick and in pain, you are getting blocked, and the Lord is allowing circumstances to frustrate you. He is giving you dreams and even touching you in a way that you really feel the weight and the pain of it. He is saying, "I am for you. I am chasing you down. We still have a great plan ahead. You still have a lot of things that you and I can do together. If I quit doing this, you are in big trouble. Sometimes some of the big ministries get exposed and we think, "Oh how tragic." It would be far more tragic if they did not get exposed and the Lord says, "No, go do it. I will leave you alone. I will even let your ministry continue to grow." That is really, really, really bad from the heavenly perspective.

Idolatry

He says, "You allowed that woman Jezebel to teach and seduce my servants to commit sexual immorality and eat things sacrificed to idols" (Rev.2:20). There are two things here. Right now, we are not that focused on the idol thing. The idol thing is going to emerge in the earth. The spirit of Jezebel is the spirit of immorality in the physical realm, and idolatry is to actually interact with demons. It is the quest for the transcendent. We look around in the western world and think, "Idols? How can they bow before that stone and talk to it. That seems so dumb." Well, it was not exactly like that. Demons really appeared and made things happen. They appeared as angels. Spirit beings would appear and power would be released.

There is such a quest for the spirit to be exhilarated with power, which one of the major strongholds worldwide before the Lord returns will be, that the westerners will be buying into idolatry and sorcery. It will look different and be far more sophisticated, but it will be dynamic interaction with the spirit realm. That is what idolatry is. That is what Jezebel was into. Interaction in the spirit realm out of the will of God and interaction in the sexual realm out of the will of God. Those were the two things. Interaction in the spirit realm, we can see it mounting, but it is not at the level yet that it is going to be.

Satan's Two-Fold Strategy

The first line of attack on a global level is to weaken the morals of the planet with immorality. Then the idolatry—the demon encounters—will increase and you can be sure that in the vast majority of these demon encounters, Satan will appear as an angel of light. They will think, "That was awesome, that really worked." The immorality will set up the situation. The touching of the body in immorality will open the door for people to long for their spirit to be exhilarated in illegal ways. Bringing the two together will bring them into depths of darkness that we cannot fully grasp. That is the two-fold strategy of Satan: to bring this longing for transcendence and to allow the spirit realm—the realm of demons—to mix with the realm of immorality, through drugs, through mind altering substances, whether it is alcohol or higher level drugs—mind altering substances—so that immorality and sorcery have a far greater convergence together in the human experience. That, in a paragraph, is the spirit of Jezebel. It really is. I see this mounting up fiercely in our nation right now. I mean, the sorcery thing, we see whispers and it is growing. But the immorality, the other thing, is growing so rapidly.

Pornography

The main operation of the spirit of Jezebel in our nation is pornography. Again, the ones who are most responsible are the ones that are producing it and promoting it, yes, and also those who are partaking of it and obviously very seriously involved. When I think of these billionaire guys, whoever they are in the earth, they are going to stand before God one day and give an answer for how they have corrupted an entire generation. This immorality will open the door straight into the realm of the spirit. When a person's morals are reduced and their conscience is defiled, and their conscience is seared, the door into the spirit realm is far easier to get through. That is the point. That is the great point of the immorality surge from hell. The point is not that the enemy is just trying to get us distracted. He wants our spirits dulled, our consciences seared, so that we easily step over the line. I am saying that multitudes in the church will easily step over the line into the spirit realm, into the dark realm of the spirit. Their spirits will be exhilarated through mind altering substances and they will be so accustomed to and so comfortable with immorality at that time. There is only one answer, the end-time prayer movement under the leadership of Jesus and the power of God breaking in. The eyes of fire are the other expression of it.

The Woman Jezebel

This woman, Jezebel, was an actual lady. She is not just a symbolic figure. Was her name actually Jezebel? I don't know. You cannot know for sure. . But they all knew who she was. And the name she was operating under depicted clearly the spirit in which she was moving. It is a spirit of immorality and it is a spirit of sorcery. I do not want us to lose sight of this and reduce this to a control spirit. Sorcery is far more than that. I am talking about a high level encounter with demon spirits. If it is a control spirit, we reduce it to a person who has a personality that bugs us. Then that is what Jezebel is and we are off the hook. Beloved, this thing is staring right down at the body of Christ, straight across America. This thing is so huge. We are all being confronted with it. Not just people who are a little pushy in their personalities. This is real and this is big. The Lord is serious about confronting it.

Saving a Nation

When I hear the voices in America—they do exist by the glory of God, but they almost do not exist. Is anybody crying out against this in the land? Will you? There are a few that we know of. However, God has His men and women all over America. It is thousands, but we need millions. We don't have millions who are crying out in the body of Christ but thousands are. I don't want to minimize the beauty of that. What I want to do is stir us up. The sin was that they tolerated her or they allowed her teaching. One translation says tolerated, another says allowed. "You allow her to go uncontested." "Our church is not into that kind of stuff." You cannot be into Jesus and be silent on this subject. I am not talking about an angry spirit, because you have been wounded somewhere. Everybody has been wounded by somebody bringing pain to the life of a family, related to some expression of immorality. It is not enough to just be wounded by somebody near you who engaged in immorality, so you are mad at it and lashing out. That is not going to solve the problem. We are talking about a tender, clear, bold, anointed voice against this spirit. Because it will save the people, and not just get something off of our chests. It is saving a nation. I look at so many people who are wrecking their lives with immorality. The Lord wants us to feel tenderness towards them, even though they have caused a lot of pain. Not figuring out how we can pound them, but figuring out a way for them to make sense of their life in the grace of God.

Out of that spirit, we have to reach into the bridal paradigm. Looking through the lens of the bride of Christ and talking about a God who desires them. We need to tell them, that they have not gone too far. They do not need to give up and give in. God is waiting right now. All they need to do is agree with Him and they will get a brand new start. Even these top pornography guys.

Salvation of the Lost

In some of our prayer meetings, one of the things we must pray for regularly is human trafficking. I have a passion for this. I want to see these evil men, who have these women trapped in cages in basements, these evil men with demons, get so gloriously converted, that they become apostles, who are filled with tears because they love Him. The power of God is on them and they transform a nation. How is that for justice? Well, because God paid the price. My point is, that when we are reaching for these guys who are steeped in iniquity, they might be the next apostle. That gal might be the next apostle or prophetess; you just don't know who she is. "Yeah, but she is such a witch." "I know, but that it is not bigger than the grace of God. What if she is a great prophetess a moment away? Let's go after her and see what the Lord will give us." My point is that we are not writing them off. I am talking about the silence of the church. On the other hand, what we do not want to do is go in the other direction and say, "We are all going to be vocal," but we are angry in being vocal. No, it is the cry for the soul of a nation. It is the cry for the soul of an individual, and the church in a generation. That is what we are fighting for and we are doing it as people who have received outrageous forgiveness. We do not forget what the score is in our life which nobody knows. We cannot forget that.

The Old Testament and the New Testament Jezebel

Well, Jezebel in the Old Testament and Jezebel in the New Testament were two completely different ladies, but they operated in the same spirit. It was immorality and spiritual power, sorcery. Their spirits were exhilarated by power. I am not just talking about having a control spirit, they encountered a transcendent dimension in the demonic realm and they were into it. That is what these Jezebels were about. Here is what the Old Testament Jezebel did: she hated Elijah and wanted to kill the prophets. The New Testament Jezebel is killing the prophets too, by dulling their spirits through pornography and immorality. She is not killing them with a sword like the Old Testament Jezebel. The New Testament Jezebel is killing them by dulling their spirits and defiling their consciences.

Prayer of Repentance for allowing the Spirit of Jezebel to Operate in our Churches

The Church of Thyatira - **We repent for allowing the spirit of Jezebel to operate in our lives.** (Worshipping false gods of immorality and sorcery) This happens as we look to satisfy the desire for sexual intimacy and spiritual power unlawfully, through sexual immorality and the worship of demon spirits, through the worship of position and authority in his body, the church. These spirits are manifested in the world through drugs, illicit sex and all types of counterfeit power surges, and in the Church it can come on us as a result of preaching and teaching as a Pastor or leader in Christ's body with the wrong motives, and heart. This is produced many times through a spirit of performance in the church, as well as assuming counterfeit authority. This spirit is also produced through lusting after position in society (political office, etc), and doing whatever is necessary to obtain those offices and positions. Lord we turn from looking to vain and worthless things to satisfy a desire for illegitimate intimacy. We turn from looking to position and authority in ministry, looking for success and fulfillment through leading and building your Church with the wrong motives. We turn to seeking purity of motives and morality, taking a purity covenant with you, and with our wives and children as our accountability partners.

CHAPTER 7

PURITY STEP #5 - CHURCH OF SARDIS
Repentance from not watching in Prayer to strengthen the things that are ready to die

> *Rev 3:1 And unto the angel of the church in Sardis write; These things saith he that hath the seven Spirits of God, and the seven stars; I know thy works, that thou hast a name that thou livest, and art dead. 2Be watchful, and strengthen the things which remain, that are ready to die: for I have not found thy works perfect before me. 3 Remember therefore how thou hast received and heard, and hold fast, and repent. If therefore thou shalt not watch, I will come on thee as a thief, and thou shalt not know what hour I will come upon thee. 6 He that hath an ear, let him hear what the Spirit saith unto the churches.*

The Primary Message

This church was known for its lively devotion to Jesus that was well established about forty years earlier (52-55 AD) in the great Ephesians revival that swept through all Asia (Acts 19-20). They were deeply touched in this revival and became well known of it. However, over time they became spiritually dead. They lived on their past reputation established decades in the revival.

> *9 Paul...reasoning daily in the school of Tyrannus. 10 And this continued for two years, so that all who dwelt in Asia heard the word of the Lord... (Acts 19:9-10)*

28. Take heed to yourselves...29 I know this, that after my departure savage wolves will come in among you...30 From among yourselves men will rise up, speaking perverse things, to draw away the disciples after themselves. 31 Therefore watch, and remember that for three years I did not cease to warn everyone night and day with tears. (Acts 20:28-31)

The Church at Sardis had no external enemies who persecuted them nor did they have internal enemies of false teachers who promoted immorality like Pergamos and Thyatira. Their problems (like in Laodicea) were self-imposed, they failed to remember the past of How Jesus touched them and how they responded in radical devotion. In other words, how alive one can be in God. Sardis was a wealthy city that boasted of being impregnable because of its topography suited for military defense. Sardis was devoted to the worship of the mother-goddess Cybele.

Exhortation to Respond (With a Warning)

2 Be watchful, and strengthen the things which remain, that are ready to die...3 Remember therefore how you have received and heard; hold fast and repent. Therefore if you will not watch, I will come upon you as a thief, and you will not know what hour I will come upon you. (Rev. 3:2-3)

The Lord compares His coming as "coming like a thief" to individuals and churches. He is not a thief but His coming to us is "like a thief." This is a proverbial expression that indicates that He comes to us at an unexpected time and in a way that we will **suffer the loss that we could have avoided** if we would have been watching. Jesus never called Himself a thief but calls the devil one (Jn. 10:10). We can "stop a thief from robbing us simply by watching." The lack of watching is what allows a thief to bring loss to one's life. Jesus comes in three ways. First, He comes in His eschatological Second Coming to Rapture the Church. Second, His coming for us at the time of physical death. Third, He comes to us during our life at "strategic times" to either promote us or to demote us. Jesus comes to us at "strategic times" to either promote us (by releasing a season of increase in the grace of God) or to demote us (by bringing us under a season of divine discipline). When He comes, He requires a response of faithfulness. If we are not found faithful then we are responsible for "suffering loss." Be watchful – cultivate a lifestyle of prayer, fasting and obedience or to sustain a lifestyle of encountering Jesus. This is the primary exhortation Jesus gives the Church in preparing us in the End-Times (Mt. 24:42-43; 25:13; Mk. 13:33-38; Lk 21:36; Rev. 3:3; 16:15). Paul's also exhorted the Church to "watch" (Acts 20:31; 1 Cor. 16:13; 1 Thes. 5:2-4, 6).

> 33 *Watch and pray; for you do not know when the time is….35 Watch therefore, for you do not know when the master of the house is coming… 37 I say to all: Watch! (Mk. 13:33-37)*

A House of Prayer or a Den of Thieves

Jesus said in Mark 11:17 *Is it not written, My house shall be called of all nations the house prayer? But ye have made it a den of thieves.* I believe that in this verse what Jesus was saying is, when we don't make our houses, houses of prayer, we make our house conducive and susceptible for the thief to come in and steal, kill, and destroy. We make our churches conducive and susceptible for the thief to come in and steal, kill and destroy our doctrines, our values, and our faith. There is an atmosphere and environment that is right for the devil to come into our Churches, our homes, families, and finances and steal, kill, and destroy. There is an atmosphere and environment that conducive for the devil to come into our churches and steal the tenets of our faith, our revelation, wisdom and understanding concerning the end-times and the coming of the Lord. It is the atmosphere and environment of prayerlessness. *When we are not a praying church, we are playing church.* When we are playing when we should be praying, we are open for the thief to come in the house. We make the house a den of thieves.

A den for thieves means our house is full of devils living amongst us waiting to take advantage of our prayerlessness to implement their long term strategies of death and destruction of our destinies and callings in God. They do this through deceptive doctrines, strife, envy, jealousy, backbiting, fornication, adultery, etc living in an atmosphere that breeds its growth and spreads amongst us. I believe this is cause of deceptive doctrines that have led the church from *a house of Prayer to a house of Stair*, where we've been staring into the clouds waiting for Jesus to return, instead of praying and preparing the way for His return. In Acts 1:11 the angels spoke to the disciples what I believe is what should be spoken to the church of the last 100 years *Men of Galilee, why stand here looking into the sky? Then they returned to Jerusalem…. And when they arrived they went up to an upper room…. And they all joined together constantly in prayer.*

The Watchmen's Warning

Ezekiel 33:2-4 *Son of man, speak to the children of thy people, and say unto them, When I bring the sword upon a land, if the people of the land take a man of their coasts. And set him for their watchman: If when he seeth the sword come upon the land, he blow the trumpet, and warn the people; Then whosoever heareth the sound of the*

> *trumpet, and takes not warning; if the sword come,*
> *and take him away, his blood shall be upon his own*
> *head.*

To be a house of prayer requires the church to be watchmen in the earth against destructive doctrines of devils, and teachings that are compromising in nature, and for the coming of mysteries and revelations of God that must be heralded in the earth to prepare the church for the unique dynamics of the end times. *Mar 11:17 And he taught, saying unto them, Is it not written, My house shall be called of all nations the house of prayer? but ye have made it a den of thieves.*

We must understand what it means to be a "Watchman." To watch in prayer is to set oneself up as a Watchman on the wall of a community, a group of people or city, looking for anything or anyone that may be coming toward the city for good or for bad. In the days of old, watchmen were placed on the walls of fortified cities to warn of attacking armies that would be coming to overtake the city. They would sound the alarm for war and prepare the armies to fight against their enemies. Watchmen also would watch for runners of news from the battlefield or from neighboring towns and villages. There would be runners of good news and runners of bad news, and the watchmen would recognize the runners of good news and the runners of bad news.

Watchmen on the Wall to Warn Against the Coming End-Time Events

As we come closer and closer to coming of the Lord the prayer movement is being raised up to establish watchmen on the wall to warn against the coming end-time events and to combat the deceptions and enemy infiltrations of the past centuries of theological end-time teachings, that have emboldened the body of Christ in her prayerlessness. This increasing movement of prayer that will position the church for the unique dynamics of the end-times and the coming of the Lord are being established on the foundations of the values of intimacy with the Lord, the First commandments of Loving the Lord with all our heart, soul, mind and strength being restored to first place in the Church, and on the teachings of Historical Pre-millennialism with a victorious church that establishes God's purposes and plans in the earth as we come to the end of the age and the coming of the Lord.

How We Went from Watching in Prayer to Watching the Air

Why has the church of the last 100 years gone from watching in prayer to the passivity of watching the air? Because we have allowed deceptive doctrines into our churches concerning the end-times that has turned us from houses of prayer preparing for the battle of the ages, to houses that stare into the air in fear, hoping to be snatched away from trouble and tribulation at the end of the age. We must re-establish prayer watches that watch for the enemy that comes to keep our churches weak, passive and star-gazing, and we must reclaim the proper biblical view of the end-times so that we might rightly view our responsibility as the church at the end of the age.

It Is Important To Have a Biblical View of the End Times

It is important to have a biblical perspective on the end times. What we believe about the end times greatly affects how we approach the work of the kingdom. Ideas have consequences. I do not ask anyone to accept my views, rather I urge you to think for yourself. Truth is never hurt by careful scrutiny, but rather it is confirmed. We must boldly challenge all the ideas that are being taught and refuse any that we cannot clearly see in Scripture for ourselves.

> *[11]They [Bereans] received the word with all readiness, and <u>searched</u> the Scriptures daily to <u>find out</u> whether <u>these things were so</u>. (Acts 17:11)*

We honor the godliness and wisdom of many who uphold different views, but some errors in understanding will leave many unprepared and even offended at Jesus in the end-time pressures. The most controversial point that I hold to is that the Church will be raptured after going through the tribulation in great victory. This differs from the pre-tribulation rapture view that teaches that the Church will be raptured at any moment, missing the end-time revival and crisis.

There are several popular end-time views taught today. One is ***too pessimistic*** (dispensational pre-millennialism) with its pre-tribulation rapture. In total contrast, another view is ***too optimistic*** (postmillennialism) with its total Christianizing of all society before Jesus returns. This view claims that things will mostly get better. This overly optimistic view will lead to confusion and disappointment. *The power and promises of God will be released in <u>fullness</u> in the Millennium, yet are still released <u>in part</u> in this age and in greater measures as we get closer to Jesus' return.*

I hold to the ***historic premillennial*** view of the end times with a post-tribulation rapture and victorious praying Church emphasized (Eph. 5:27; Rev. 19:7). The Church will be victorious in love with power during the most dramatic time in history. This view gives us confidence and urgency to <u>dynamically participate</u> with Jesus now and in the coming revival. The harvest of righteousness and of sin will **both** come to fullness at the end of the age resulting in the greatest outpouring of the Spirit and the greatest crisis in history—the tribulation.

> *[30]Let <u>both</u> [wheat and tares] grow <u>together</u> until the harvest... (Mt. 13:30)*

> *[11]For the Day of the LORD is <u>great</u> and <u>very terrible</u>; who can endure it? (Joel 2:11)*

<u>Many unique dynamics will occur in Jesus' end-time plan</u> as He transitions the earth from this present age to the age to come and drives evil off the earth forever. He has a plan to intervene to confront oppression and corruption in a way that He has never done before (Rev. 19:2). God's judgments will remove all that hinders love so that multitudes are saved and mature in love. He uses the <u>least severe</u> means to reach the <u>greatest number</u> of people at the <u>deepest level</u> of love.

The Millennial Kingdom

The Millennium is a literal 1,000-year period in which Jesus will rule the whole world from Jerusalem in righteousness, peace, and prosperity (Rev. 20:1-6). Jesus will govern in partnership with resurrected saints to establish a biblically-based social order (Mt. 19:28; 25:23; Lk. 19:17-19; 22:29-30; 1 Cor. 6:2-3; 2 Tim. 2:12; Rom. 8:17; Rev. 2:26-27; 3:21; 5:10; 20:4-6).

> *[4]They lived and <u>reigned with Christ for a thousand years</u>...[6]They shall be priests of God and of Christ, and shall <u>reign with Him a thousand years</u>. (Rev. 20:4-6)*

The kingdom of God will be openly manifest worldwide, affecting every sphere of life (politics, economy, education, agriculture, media, technology, environment, social institutions, etc.). This period of worldwide blessing will be initiated by Jesus' second coming (Isa. 2:1-4; 9:6-9; 11:1-16; 65:17-25; Ps. 2; 110; Mt. 6:10; 17:11; 19:28; 28:19; Acts 1:6; 3:21; Rev. 20:1-6).

Historic Pre-millennialism mostly teach a post-tribulation rapture (Jesus will return "after" the tribulation) and a literal interpretation of end-time prophecy and honor God's purpose for Israel. **Dispensational Pre-millennialism** teach a pre-tribulation rapture (Jesus will return "before" the tribulation) and the literal interpretation of end-time prophecy and honor God's purpose for Israel. Most do not believe that the Church will be used to transform parts of society, operate in the gifts of the Spirit or win the end-time harvest. This is a new theology that was systematized in the 1830s by John Darby. It is called *dispensational* because it teaches that God has related differently to His people in seven dispensations of history. It includes: (1) two covenants of salvation (Israel and the Church); (2) a literal interpretation of Scripture; (3) pre-millennial views; (4) pre-tribulation; (5) imminency that sees the possibility of an "any moment" rapture.

Today, some who hold dispensational views reject some of the early beliefs of their movement. *Classical Dispensationalism* (1850–1950s) sees the Church is a parenthesis in salvation history. *Revised Dispensationalism* (1950–1980s) rejects the idea of two new covenants (for Israel and the Church), but sees their distinction in eternity. *Progressive Dispensationalism* (1980s–present) refers to the "progressive" relationship of the successive dispensations to one another.

Dispensational Pre-millennialism

The strength of the Dispensational Pre-millennialist view is found in its literal interpretation of end-time prophecy and in embracing God's purpose for Israel in the end times. **Its weakness** is that most who hold this view do not believe that the Church will be used to transform parts of society, or that it will operate in the gifts of the Spirit, or be on earth during the tribulation to finish winning the harvest.

It sees two new covenants pertaining to salvation—one for Israel and one for the Church. (Dispensationalists have differing views on this). One weakness common to dispensationalists is in teaching on the pre-tribulation rapture of the Church. Dispensational pre-millennialism is an overly pessimistic eschatology. The common response is **_escapism_** *(why prepare and work hard if we will soon be raptured)* along with **_fatalism_** and defeatism *(society cannot be changed so why try)*. The <u>doctrine of eminency</u> (Jesus returning at any moment) does not emphasize the need for a long-term plan to impact society or for Gentile believers to provoke Israel to jealousy and salvation by standing with them in persecution during the tribulation. Some with this view see the Church's mandate as being like a <u>life raft</u>, limited to delivering people from drowning (preaching only salvation), while abdicating our kingdom responsibility to call society out of darkness. This view can lead to a lazy disengagement. Yet, some dispensationalist churches are very active in soul-winning.

Historic Pre-millennialism: The Traditional View

The strength of this view is found in its literal interpretation of end-time prophecy, in preparing the Church for future persecution, and in our responsibility to provoke Israel to salvation.

Its weakness is that some who hold this view do not believe that the Church will grow strong in prayer that will result in the great harvest and in end-time victory and power as she functions in her bridal identity (Rev. 22:17). Note: some with this view do see a victorious praying Church.

Historic Pre-millennialism with a Victorious Church

The strength of this view is found in combining the biblical strengths of postmillennialism and amillennialism with historic pre-millennialism and the call to victory and wholeheartedness.

A victorious Church: attains to unity, intimacy, and maturity, resulting in the greatest revival in history (Eph. 4:13). This prophetic praying Church will walk in great power as it is used to bring in the end-time harvest and to transform society in various places.

A wholehearted Church: walks in "Sermon on the Mount lifestyles" of self-denial and serving, giving, blessing, praying, and fasting as seen in the New Testament Church (Mt. 5-7). This lifestyle will be energized by encountering Jesus as the Bridegroom God (Rev. 22:17).

A relevant Church: sees the ***continuity*** of some of our labors in impacting society now (righteous legislation, education, etc.) with the work of Jesus in the Millennium. All that is unrighteous will be dismantled and then re-established in righteousness in the Millennium. However, righteous legislation in society in this age will not need to be replaced. Works in society built on godliness and justice will last beyond the shaking of the tribulation judgments.

Two Common Objections to Historic Pre-millennialism

Some claim that the <u>Holy Spirit is the restrainer</u> that is removed when the Church is raptured. Paul prophesied the removal of a "someone" or "something" that restrains the Antichrist from being revealed (2 Thes. 2:6-8). Paul described the restrainer of the increase of sin and the release of the Antichrist as a "what" (neuter gender in 2:6) and as a "He" (masculine gender in 2:7). Paul taught that governing authorities are appointed by God to restrain evil (Rom. 13:1-4). I believe the restraining force that is removed is a combination of a "what," which I believe to be the existence of national governments that will not allow the Antichrist's government to emerge, and a "He," which I believe to be God and His sovereign decree to bring the ten-nation confederation into unity with the Antichrist (Rev. 17:17).

Some claim that we will not go through the Tribulation because "<u>we are not appointed unto wrath</u>" (1 Thes. 5:9). It is true—the Church is *not* appointed to wrath. The wrath of God in the tribulation will be released to destroy the Antichrist's empire, not the Church.

What is the Rapture

What is the rapture? The rapture describes what happens to the saints worldwide when Jesus appears in the sky at His Second Coming.

> *For the Lord will descend from heaven with a shout, with the voice of an archangel, and with the trumpet of God. And the dead in Christ will rise first. Then we who are alive and remain shall be caught up together with them in the clouds to meet the Lord in the air... (1 Thes. 4:16-17)*

The Greek words for "caught up" are arpazw harpazo (Strong's 726). This means, "to seize, catch (away, up), pluck, pull, take (by force), gather." Latin – In Latin the term "caught up" is translated rapio. It is from rapio that we get the word rapture. Paul understood that being caught up meant meeting Jesus in the air. The Greek word parousia is the most popular word used to describe Jesus' Second Coming.

This idea of being caught up to meet Jesus in the air, from a post-tribulation perspective, has been questioned as illogical since Jesus is returning to the earth after the tribulation. Historically this word was commonly used to describe the visit of a king to a city in his domain. As the king would approach the city he would be met some distance outside of the town by a select group of dignitaries and close relatives, who would then accompany him in his procession through the city gates to be seen by the resident population. The historical usage of the word parousia clearly pictures what the New Testament describes as occurring at the Second Coming. Believers, both those who have died and those who are still living, will "meet the Lord in the air" (1 Thess. 4:17) and accompany Him on the last part of his journey back to earth.

When the Rapture will Occur

The big question that has been debated for the better part of the last 100 years is: when will the rapture take place? This is the question I hope to answer. For many, the answer to this question is a foregone conclusion. Typically people's view differs based on what stream of the Body of Christ in which they were raised. I grew up in traditional Pentecostal church so my view was shaped by the pre-tribulation perspective. In fact, so much so, that it even affected the way I interpreted my vision and dreams in God. One night I had a dream that I was in the midst of the Great Tribulation. I was given a mandate to start a grocery store to feed Christians food during the great tribulation.. When I awoke I was

93

terrified because I thought, "Oh no, I must be going to fall away from the Lord in the future, and be left behind." There is almost a universal conviction among pre-millennial scholars that the final week of Daniel is the time frame that concludes this age. In other words, human history in this age will end with a unique seven-year period of time. The discussion concerning the rapture involves discerning at what point before, during, or after this seven years the rapture occurs.

Views on the rapture

There are four different views on the timing of the rapture according to those who subscribe to pre-millennial eschatology.

Pre-tribulation – Views the rapture as occurring seven years before Jesus' Second Coming.

Mid-tribulation – Views the rapture as occurring 3 ½ years before Jesus' Second Coming.

Pre-wrath – Views the rapture as occurring at an undefined period of time after the 3½-year mark of the Tribulation and before the end of the Tribulation. This view sees the rapture as occurring at the sixth seal in the book of Revelation (Rev. 6:12-17).

Post-tribulation – Views the rapture as occurring after the Tribulation at the Second Coming of Jesus.

How many "comings" of Jesus and "resurrections" of the saints? – Three of these views (pre-trib, mid-trib, and pre-wrath) stand or fall on the basis of two basic premises: 1) Are there two Second Comings of Christ? 2) Are there two resurrections of the saints? If it can be accurately shown that there are, then distinguishing when the rapture occurs would be extremely difficult, and basically be an arbitrary judgment. If there is not then these views are inconclusive and ultimately the product of mere speculation. In my observation and understanding of Scripture there is no explicit evidence to support the conclusion that there are two, separate Second Coming events, nor two resurrections of the saints. The best place for us to begin to answer the question "when does the rapture occur?" is by identifying what we know to be true about the Second Coming and the rapture. The five truths I am going to present directly contrast three of the four rapture views.

The Second Coming is a Singular Event Occurring After the Tribulation

"Immediately after the tribulation of those days the sun will be darkened, and the moon will not give its light; the stars will fall from heaven, and the powers of the heavens will be shaken. Then the sign of the Son of Man will appear in heaven, and then all the tribes of the earth will mourn, and they will see the Son of Man coming on the clouds of heaven with power and great glory. And He will send His angels with a great sound of a trumpet, and they will gather together His elect from the four winds, from one end of heaven to the other." – Mt.24:29-31

Jesus describes His Second Coming as a singular event occurring after the tribulation. At no point in His teaching ministry does he ever reference another time frame for His return. After His resurrection Jesus spent forty days with His disciples. When He finally ascended into heaven two angels appeared to the disciples and informed them: "This same Jesus, who was taken up from you into heaven, will so come in like manner as you saw Him go into heaven." (Acts 1:11) The angels described a singular event in which Jesus would come back from heaven to the earth. Some point to 1 Thes. 4:15-18 to validate a view that Jesus Christ returns momentarily in the sky to rapture the church seven years before His Second Coming. However, there is no doubt that Paul's views were formed by Christ's teachings. If he was introducing a new view concerning a subject as important as an entirely separate Second Coming event, I imagine he would have said so. Paul's teaching harmonizes perfectly with what Jesus taught in the Olivet Discourse.

> *For this we say to you by the word of the Lord, that we who are alive, and remain [perileipomenoi] until the coming of the Lord will by no means precede those who are asleep. For the Lord Himself will descend from heaven with a shout, with the voice of an archangel, and with the trumpet of God. And the dead in Christ will rise first. Then we who are alive and remain [perileipomenoi] shall be caught up together with them in the clouds to meet the Lord in the air. And thus we shall always be with the Lord. Therefore comfort one another with these words. – 1 Thes. 4:15-18.*

Nowhere in the text is precedence given for a time frame other than the one already established by Jesus. Consider the parallels in the two passages: In Matthew 24 we see that Christ is descending from heaven with angels and a trumpet gathering together His followers. In 1Thess 4 we see that Christ is descending from heaven with angels and a trumpet, gathering together His followers. The noun used for the word "come" (parousia) in the NT means arrival or presence. The verb tense of this word implies continuous and progressive action. When Jesus returns, He is coming to establish His manifest presence and initiate an indefinite mission upon the earth.

Any position subscribing to a view that necessitates two Second Coming events is rooted in theory not Scripture. This is an important distinction to make. Nowhere does the Bible delineate between two separate Second Coming events. However the Bible does emphatically describe one event, which occurs after the Tribulation, not at any point before it.

The Rapture Occurs After the Tribulation

> *"Immediately after the tribulation of those days the sun will be darkened, and the moon will not give its light; the stars will fall from heaven, and the powers of the heavens will be shaken. Then the sign of the Son of Man will appear in heaven, and then all the tribes of the earth will mourn, and they will see the Son of Man coming on the clouds of heaven with power and great glory. And He will send His angels with a great sound of a trumpet, and they will gather (episynago) together His elect from the four winds, from one end of heaven to the other."* –
> Mt. 24:29-31

Jesus describes the rapture as an event that is synonymous with His Second Coming. The apostle Paul also describes the Second Coming and the rapture as one synonymous event.

> *"Now, brethren, concerning the coming of our Lord Jesus Christ and our gathering (episynago) together to Him..."* – 2 Thes. 2:1

Both Jesus and Paul use the same word for "gather," episynago. The only explicit time frame given to understand the return of Christ and rapture of the saints is "after the tribulation." If the rapture occurs after the tribulation what does that mean? It means the Church is here during the tribulation. Jesus, in fact, prefigures the presence of believers during the tribulation.

> *"Therefore when you see the 'abomination of desolation'... And pray that your flight may not be in the winter or on the Sabbath. For then there will be great tribulation, since has not been since the beginning of the world until this time, no, nor ever shall be... Then if anyone says to you, 'Look, here is the Christ!' or 'There!' do not believe it... Therefore if they say to you, 'Look, He is in the desert!' do not go out... For as the lightning comes from the east and flashes to the west, so also will the coming of the Son of Man be." (Mt. 24:15,20-21, 23, 26-27)*

The clear emphasis of Jesus' teaching prefigured the presence of believers on earth during the Great Tribulation. Dispensationalists would speculate that Jesus was speaking to Jews here, and so it is the Jews who will be present during the tribulation, while the Church has been raptured. If one is consistent with their logic then they must at least acknowledge it is "believing" Jews who Jesus is speaking to. So are we now meant to understand that though the church has been raptured, Jewish believers are left behind because of their ethnicity? Are they then not members of the Church? This train of logic is a theological train wreck. I do not have time in this chapter to develop how preposterous this scenario is. The fact is that Jesus is preparing the leaders of His Church with important information pertaining to their survival during the great tribulation. Believers are also pictured as present during the Great Tribulation throughout the book of Revelation. Once again dispensationalists would redefine this truth by pointing out that though the term "saints" is used, the word "ecclesia" or Church is not used in Rev. 4-19. Their conclusion then is that the Church must not be here and that the saints that are written about are a new group of believers who were saved during the Tribulation but are not members of the Church. Once again the logic employed here is not consistent. Revelation 4-19 illustrates what is occurring on earth AND in heaven. If the term ecclesia is the technical word that we use to decipher the presence or lack thereof of the church, and the conclusion is that since ecclesia isn't used in Rev. 4-19 the Church cannot be on the earth, then doesn't it stand to reason that the Church cannot be in heaven either? This presents an irreconcilable quandary, and therefore cannot be considered tenable.

Indeed the term ecclesia is not the technical word by which we decipher the presence of the Church. In fact six NT epistles do not use the term ecclesia (2 Tim., Titus, 1 & 2 Peter, 2 John, and Jude) but do use the term saints, a term used throughout the book of Revelation. Even more striking, the word Church is also missing from those passages directly dealing with the rapture when Christians see Jesus again (Jn. 14:1; 1 Cor. 15; 1 Thes. 4-5). It is not even in the description of the new heaven and new earth or the New Jerusalem (Rev. 21-22).

The idea that the Church is here during the Tribulation has been cause for opposition by the pre-trib camp on another front as well. They present the "doctrine of comfort" as reassurance that the saints will not endure the Tribulation because it is a time of God's wrath. I will give a summary response to this because I do not have time in this chapter to belabor the technical implications involving ecclesiology verses soteriology, which are massive. In regards to tribulation, believers are never promised that they will be kept from tribulation, but rather that they will go through it:

> *...In the world you will have tribulation... – Jn. 16:33*

> *...They will deliver you up to tribulation and kill you,*

and you will be hated by all nations for My name's sake. – Mt. 24:9

Yes and all who desire to live godly in Christ Jesus will suffer persecution. – 2 Tim. 3:12

...No one should be shaken by these afflictions; for you yourselves know that we are appointed to this. For, in fact, we told you before when we were with you that we would suffer tribulation, just as it happened, and you know. – 1 Thess. 3:3-4

And when they had preached the gospel to that city and made many disciples, exhorting them to continue in the faith, and saying, "We must through many tribulations enter the kingdom of God." – Acts 14:22

Beloved, do not think it strange concerning the fiery trial which is to try you, as though some strange thing happened to you. – 1 Pet. 4:12

In regards to the doctrine of comfort, I agree and affirm that God is a God of comfort, but again, I think the pre-trib camp has made an unbiblical application of this paradigm.

Blessed be the God and Father of our Lord Jesus Christ, the Father of all comfort, who comforts us in all our tribulation, which we might be able to comfort those who are in any trouble with the comfort with which we ourselves are comforted by God. For as the sufferings of Christ abound in us, so our consolation also abounds through Christ. ... And our hope for you is steadfast, because we know that as you are partakers of the sufferings, so also

> *you will partake of the consolation. – 2 Cor. 2-5, 7*
> *"These things I have spoken to you, that in Me you may have peace. In the world you will have tribulation; but be of good cheer, I have overcome the world." – Jn. 16:33*

In regards to the subject of God's wrath – Foundational to the pre-tribulation rapture view is the belief that the Church must be raptured before the Tribulation begins because Christians are not appointed unto wrath. The pre-tribulation view holds that the present age is characterized by grace and that the Tribulation is characterized by wrath, therefore the Church cannot be here during the Tribulation. Walvoord clarified this position: "The only way one could be kept from that day of wrath would be to be delivered beforehand." There are several points in this view that require discussion. First of all, Romans 1 reveals that God's wrath is already being revealed. The difference between the wrath manifested now and the great tribulation is one of degree not kind. It is a fabrication of Scripture to suggest that we are currently in an age of grace and yet the Tribulation is one of wrath. Evidences of God's grace and His wrath permeate history and will continue to all the way through the Great Tribulation at which time the largest harvest of souls in history will take place. Does this mean that Christians are appointed to wrath? Absolutely not!

> *For God did not appoint us to wrath, but to obtain salvation through our Lord Jesus Christ... - 1 Thess. 5:9*
> *Much more then, having now been justified by His blood, we shall be saved from wrath through Him. – Rom. 5:9*

The bible teaches the wrath of God is directed toward the wicked, not the righteous. (Rev. 14:9-11; Eph. 5:6*)*

> *...Because of these things the wrath of God is coming upon the sons of disobedience. – Eph. 5:6*

The difference in the two views concerns God's method of deliverance from wrath. The biblical precedence for the deliverance of God's people from His wrath is always through protection or redirection – never by being raptured.

Protection

In the book of Revelation we are given insight into God's method of deliverance for the righteous. In 7:3-4 144,000 are sealed, and consequently protected from the wrath of God. This is consistent with God's means of protection for His people throughout the OT, for example: the people of God in Egypt during the plagues, Rahab in the midst of the downfall of Jericho, Noah and his family in the ark during the midst of the flood, Daniel in the lions' den, and Shadrach, Meshach, and Abednego in the fiery furnace.

> *Come, my people, enter your chambers, and shut your doors behind you; hide yourself, as it were, for a little moment, until the indignation is past. For behold, the Lord comes out of His place to punish the inhabitants of the earth for their iniquity; the earth will also disclose her blood... – Isa. 26:20-21*

> *Then I saw another angel ascending from the east, having the seal of the living God. And he cried with a loud voice to the four angels to whom it was granted to harm the earth and the sea, saying, "Do not harm the earth, the sea, or the trees till we*

have sealed the servants of our God on their foreheads.– Rev.7:2-3

And in that day I will set apart the land of Goshen, in which My people dwell, that no swarms of flies shall be there, in order that you may know that I am the Lord in the midst of the land. I will make a difference between My people and your people...– Ex.8:22-23

Now the city shall be doomed by the Lord to destruction, it and all who are in it. Only Rahab the harlot shall live, she and all who are with her in the house.... – Josh. 6:17

Redirection

God directs His people away from coming judgment (Rev. 12; 18:4). When the morning dawned, the angels urged Lot to hurry, saying, "Arise, take your wife and your two daughters who are here, lest you be consumed in the punishment of the city." And while he lingered, the men took hold of his hand, his wife's hand, and the hands of his two daughters, the Lord being merciful to him, and they brought him out and set him outside the city. – Gen 19:15-16

> *And I heard another voice from heaven saying, "Come out of her, my people, lest you share in her sins, and lest you receive of her plagues. – Rev. 18:4 Then the woman fled into the wilderness, where she has a place prepared by God, that they should feed her there one thousand two hundred and sixty days... But the woman was given two wings of a great eagle, that she might fly into the wilderness to her place, where she is nourished for a time and*

Prayer of Repentance from not watching in Prayer to strengthen the things that remain

The Church of Sardis - We repent for not watching in prayer to strengthen the things that remain, allowing the thief to steal our doctrines and faith with the various teachings that seek to avoid persecution. <u>Lord, we turn to the study of these doctrines and teachings on the end-times, the rapture and the second coming of the Lord that we have let slip, and commit our lives to teach and preach what the bible teaches about the coming of the Lord as Bridegroom, King and Judge.</u>

CHAPTER 8

PURITY STEP # 6 - CHURCH OF PHILADELPHIA
The Release of the Key of David - 24hr prayer & worship to open a door in the earth no man can shut

Rev 3:7 And to the angel of the church in Philadelphia write; These things saith he that is holy, he that is true, **he that hath the key of David, he that openeth, and no man shutteth; and shutteth, and no man openeth; 8 I know thy works: behold, I have set before thee an open door, and no man can shut it: for thou hast a little strength, and hast kept my word, and hast not denied my name.** *9 Behold, I will make them of the synagogue of Satan, which say they are Jews, and are not, but do lie; behold, I will make them to come and worship before thy feet, and to know that I have loved thee.10 Because thou hast kept the word of my patience, I also will keep thee from the hour of temptation, which shall come upon all the world, to try them that dwell upon the earth. **12** Him that overcometh will I make a pillar in the temple of my God, and he shall go no more out:* **and I will write upon him the name of my God, and the name of the city of my God, which is new Jerusalem, which cometh down out of heaven from my God**: *and I will write upon him my new name. 13* **He that hath an ear, let him hear what the Spirit saith unto the churches.**

The Primary Message

In the giving of the word of the Lord to the church at Philadelphia like Smyrna, they received no rebuke but only affirmations. The Church of Philadelphia faithfully obeyed God's Word and persevered in much difficulty. Jesus' primary message developed what He promised the disciples in Jn. 14:21-23.

> 21 *He who has My commandments and keeps them, it is he who loves Me. And he who loves Me will be loved (open display of it) by My Father, and I will love him and manifest Myself to him." 22 Judas (not Iscariot) said, "Lord, how is it that You will manifest Yourself to us, and not to the world?" 23 Jesus answered and said to him, "If anyone loves Me, he will keep My word; and My Father will love him (openly display it), and We will come to him and make Our home with him." (Jn. 14:21-23)*

Isaiah 22:15-25 speaks of King Hezekiah's chief leader, Shebna being removed from his governmental position and being replaced by Eliakim. The Philadelphia Church's affirmation is based on this description. God promised to place on Eliakim's shoulder the "key to the house of David" so he could open and shut doors of authority to release kingdom activity in Hezekiah's Kingdom. This key is the tabernacle of David model of 24/7 prayer and Worship to bind Kings and Kingdoms of darkness, and to release heaven on earth.

> 22 *The key of the house of David I will lay on his (Eliakim's) shoulder; so he shall open, and no one shall shut; and he shall shut, and no one shall open...25 In that day...the peg (Eliakim's position) that is fastened in the secure place will be removed... (Isa. 22:22, 25)*

106

The Church Of Philadelphia

Ancient Philadelphia was on the site of modern day Alashehir at the juncture of trade routes. The imperial route from Rome passed through Philadelphia thus, giving it the name "the gateway to the East" making it an important financial city. It was a prosperous city.

Jesus' Revelation of Himself

> 7 *These things says He who is holy, He who is true, He who has the key of David, He who opens and no one shuts, and shuts and no one opens... (Rev. 3:7)*

This description reveals aspects of Jesus' personality and ministry. This emphasizes His care for our lives and the way He intervenes in His ministry to help those persecuted and in difficulty.

He who is holy – as a man, Jesus was holy or set apart fully to seek and obey the Father. Thus, He understands what it means to walk out costly commitments among sinful people on earth. As God, He is transcendent (wholly "other than") or infinitely superior to all. Thus, He is worth it. ***He who is true*** – reliable and genuine in His promises in Rev. 3:12 that are such extravagant ones, they seem too good to be true. Before He reveals these promises, He declares He is true.

He has the key of David

The Church of Philadelphia is one of the seven churches that did not receive a correction from the Glorified Christ of the lamp stands. I believe that this is because of the revelation and authority that they had been given of the glorified Christ having the Key of David to open a door that no man could shut. This key that David obtained was the revelation of 24/7 worship in the tabernacle of David. David received a revelation of worship around the throne and it was this revelation that was the key to David's Kingdom authority and dominion during his reign as King of Israel.

Worship on Earth like It Is in Heaven

As I stated in the introduction, I believe God is going to use 24/7 worship and prayer in the earth through his church that is returned to her eternal identity as the House of Prayer for all nations at the end of the age, to release open doors, and open heavens over whole regions in the earth at the time of Judgment and divine shaking that will be on the earth at the end of age. It is during this time, that through 24/7 worship and prayer pockets of mercy and cities of refuge will be raised up in specified regions of the earth to protect, provide and prosper Christ body during the greatest times of tribulation the world has ever known. Sacred Assemblies like the 24hr Call Detroit are God's prescribed method to either avert the judgment completely, or lessen it in a geographical region, or prepare a generation to stand without offense in the midst of the economic, environmental, military crisis that are clearly seen in Joel and passages that clearly articulate the conditions of the end of the age. Prayer meetings are God's remedy of response to impending judgment. I believe this Detroit Call as well as many of the other prayer meetings on this date last year was given not to be a one-time event, but as a prescription of what we will do during the time of the day of the Lord. God's remedy for preservation, protection and provision for his people during this coming day is night and day prayer meetings in the nations of the earth.

David's Vow

As a young man, David made a vow to dedicate his life to find a resting place or dwelling place for God. This refers to a place where an unusual measure of God's presence is manifest on earth. David's life work was to establish a dwelling place for God in Jerusalem in his generation.

> *1 LORD, remember David and all his afflictions; 2 How he swore to the LORD, and vowed to the Mighty One: 3 "Surely I will not go into the chamber of my house, or go up to the comfort of my bed; 4 I will not give sleep to my eyes...5 until I find a place for the LORD, a dwelling place for the Mighty One of Jacob"...8 Arise, O, Lord, to Your resting place. (Ps. 132:1-8)*

David vowed to live in extravagant devotion to seek the Lord with all his resources (time, talents, treasures). His vow included spending time in God's House (Ps. 27:4), fasting (Ps. 69:7-12), extravagant giving of his money (1 Chr. 22:14) and embracing God's order in worship. This vow changed history and continues today in those who embrace it. It is at the heart of the End-Time worship movement. Lord, raise up a million believers who fully walk out this vow. David's vow positioned his heart to receive insight into the worship that God seeks.

> *23 True worshipers will worship the Father in spirit and truth; for the Father is seeking such to worship Him. (Jn. 4:23)*

David received revelation of worship in God's heavenly sanctuary (1 Chr. 28:11-19).

> *96 I have seen the consummation of all perfection*

> *(God's Throne of Glory)… (Ps. 119:96.) 11. David gave his son Solomon the plans…12 for all that he had by the Spirit, of the courts of the house of the LORD…13 also for the division of the priests and the Levites, for all the work of the service of the house of the LORD…19 All this," said David, "the LORD made me understand in writing, by His hand upon me, all the works of these plans." (1 Chr. 28:11-19)*

Rev. 4-5 describes the worship order around God's Throne. Those nearest God's Throne agree with Him in 24/7 worship and intercession as the most exalted occupation in the New Jerusalem.

> *8 The 4 living creatures…do not rest day or night, saying: "Holy, holy, holy…" 10 the twenty four elders fall down…and worship Him who lives forever and ever… (Rev. 4:8-9)*
> *2 I heard a voice from heaven, like the voice of many waters, and…loud thunder. I heard the sound of harpists…3 They sang…a new song before the Throne… (Rev. 14:2-3)*

> *13 Every creature which is in heaven and on the earth…saying: "Blessing and honor…be toHim who sits on the Throne, and to the Lamb, forever and ever!" 14 The twenty-four elders fell down and worshiped Him who lives forever and ever. (Rev. 5:13-14)*

The KJV says that God "inhabits (lives in or manifests His life) in the praise of His people. David taught that when we sing praise that God inhabits (manifests His power) in that context. *3. You are…enthroned (manifest the power of Your Throne) in the praises of Israel. (Ps. 22:3)* David's revelation of heavenly worship (as seen in Psalms) is foundational to David's throne which is "political government in the spirit of the Tabernacle of David" or government based on 24/7 worship and intercession. David's government flowed forth from prophetic worship (1 Chr. 23-25). David had revelation of the spiritual impact of prophetic intercessory worship (Ps. 22:3).

> *6 Let the high praises of God be in their mouth... 7 to execute vengeance (justice) on the nations, and punishments on the peoples; 8 to bind their kings with chains...9 to execute on them the written judgment-- this honor have all His saints. (Ps. 149:6-9)*

After David became king, the first thing he did was to capture Jerusalem (2 Sam. 5:3-10). Then he gave expression to his sacred vow by setting up a worship tabernacle in Jerusalem (2 Sam. 6). David received revelation from God about establishing God's order of worship first in Jerusalem. One of the first things that Jesus will do when He rules Jerusalem is to establish worship there.

> *1 David...prepared a place for the ark of God, and pitched a tent for it...16 David spoke to the...Levites to appoint...singers accompanied by instruments of music... (1 Chr. 15:1-16)*

David put Levites before the Ark (which spoke of God's Throne and presence) to worship God.

> *1 They brought the ark...and set it in the midst of the tabernacle that David erected for it. 4 He appointed Levites (singers) to minister before the ark...to praise the Lord...37 to minister before the ark regularly, as every day's work required... (1 Chr. 16:1, 4, 37)*

David established 4,000 full-time paid musicians, 288 singers (12 x 24 = 288) and 4,000 gatekeepers. Thus, he financed about 10,000 full-time staff to facilitate worship.

> *7 The number...instructed in the songs of the Lord...who were skillful, was 288. (1 Chr. 25:7) 5 4,000 were gatekeepers, and 4,000 praised the Lord with musical instruments... (1 Chr. 23:5)*

David commanded God's people to honor the heavenly order of worship that he received by revelation because it was God's command (2 Chr. 29:25; 35:4, 15; Ezra 3:10; Neh. 12:45). These worship principles are timeless and valid today, such as establishing singers and musicians in God's House. The application of these principles would differ in each generation and culture.

> *25 Hezekiah...stationed Levites in the house of the Lord with stringed instruments... according to the commandment of David...for thus was the commandment of the Lord.(2 Chr. 29:25)*

David provided financial support so that singers could sing as a full-time occupation.

> *33 These are the singers...who lodged in the chambers, and were free from other duties; for they were employed in that work day and night. (1 Chr. 9:33)*

God's order for supporting the singers and gatekeepers was revealed to David. The storehouse was the central place to receive tithes that was under the spiritual leadership of the Lord's House. Asaph and his brothers were included in the 288 singers (12 x 24 = 288).

> *37 So he left Asaph and his brothers there before the ark of the covenant of the LORD to minister before the ark regularly, as every day's work required... (1 Chr. 16:37)*

David gave over $100 billion (according to today's prices) to God's House from his personal finances. One talent equals about 75 lbs or 1200 ounces (16 ounces in a pound). 100,000 talents weighed about 7.5 million pounds (almost 4,000 tons). At $700 an ounce, a talent of gold would be worth about $850,000. Thus, 100,000 talents of gold would be worth about $85 billion. A talent of silver at $12 an ounce is worth nearly $15,000, thus one million talents of silver (75 million pounds or almost 40,000 tons) is worth about $15 billion. *(1 Chr. 22:14)*

> *14 Indeed I have taken much trouble to prepare for the House of the LORD 100,000talents of gold ($85 billion) and 1,000,000 talents of silver ($15 billion)...*

Embracing David's Revelation of Worship in the Old Testament

Solomon established the singers according to the direction that God gave his father David.

> *14 According to the order of David his father, he (Solomon) appointed...Levites for their duties to praise...as the duty of each day required...for so David...commanded. (2 Chr. 8:14)*

Amos (about 750 BC) prophesied of the restoration of David's Tabernacle and thus to reverse the damage of Israel's apostasy. The fullness of the Tabernacle of David speaks of Jesus' Millennial government over all nations that is based on 24/7 Davidic worship and intercession.

> *11 On that day I will raise up the Tabernacle of David, which has fallen down, and repair its damages; I will raise up its ruins, and rebuild it as in the days of old… (Amos 9:11)*

When Israel went astray, God raised up spiritual reformers with a vision to restore worship as David commanded it. All of the 7 "revivals" in OT times restored Davidic worship.

Prayer of Dedication to 24/7 Prayer & Worship Ministry of the Tabernacle of David in Our Cities

<u>The Church of Philadelphia</u> - We commit to the 24/7 paradigm of the key of David as the church of Philadelphia. This church was given the keys of David to open a door that is shut, and shut doors that should not be opened. <u>We commit to establish 24/7 places of worship & prayer in the cities of the earth, culminating in Jerusalem to bind darkness and loose light in our cities</u>. This is what will enable the church to resist the compromises and the sins represented in the other churches of Asia, which are represented in the church of the end-time generation, and be able to stand before the Lord in the Great and Terrible day of the Lord.

CHAPTER 9

PURITY STEP # 7 - THE CHURCH OF LAODICEA
Repentance from being Lukewarm

*Rev 3:14 And unto the angel of the church of the Laodiceans write; These things saith the Amen, the faithful and true witness, the beginning of the creation of God;15 **I know thy works, that thou art neither cold nor hot: I would thou wert cold or hot. 16 So then because thou art lukewarm, and neither cold nor hot, I will spue thee out of my mouth.17 Because thou sayest, I am rich, and increased with goods, and have need of nothing; and knowest not that thou art wretched, and miserable, and poor, and blind, and naked:** 18 I counsel thee to buy of me gold tried in the fire, that thou mayest be rich; and white raiment, that thou mayest be clothed, and that the shame of thy nakedness do not appear; and anoint thine eyes with eyesalve, that thou mayest see. 19 As many as I love, I rebuke and chasten: be zealous therefore, and repent. 20 **Behold, I stand at the door, and knock: if any man hear my voice, and open the door, I will come in to him, and will sup with him, and he with me.** 21 To him that overcometh will I grant to sit with me in my throne, even as I also overcame, and am set down with my Father in his throne. 22 **He that hath an ear, let him hear what the Spirit saith unto the churches.***

Jesus promises the prestigious wealthy church of the Laodiceans deep fellowship and a position in His eternal Kingdom along with gold, garments and revelation. However, to receive this He required that they zealously repent of their lukewarmness in their relationship with Him. Their problem was spiritual blindness and pride that led to lukewarmness in their love for the Lord. One root problem they had came from misinterpreting why God gave them financial blessing. The Lord releases financial blessing as part of the covenant that He has made with His people. There is much emphasis on the biblical promise of receiving financial blessing from God (Deut. 28:1-14).When our finances grow faster than our heart then negative dynamics occur.

> *18. You shall remember the LORD your God, for it is He who gives you power to get wealth, that He may establish His covenant which He swore to your fathers... (Deut. 8:18)*

We must not allow financial prosperity to hinder our heart prosperity nor our heavenly treasure. The church of Smyrna was financially poor because of persecution, but was spiritually rich. The Laodiceans had the opposite condition.

> *2. I pray that you may prosper in all things and be in health, just as your soul prospers. (3 Jn. 2)*

It is more difficult for a person who is rich in money or honor to enter (experience) the kingdom. It requires much time and energy to manage increase in God given money and honor. In being preoccupied with wealth and reputation it is easy to neglect our spiritual life. The Laodiceans spoke of being financially rich without being in need of spiritual depth. Their financial increase led to losing their hunger for Jesus. This does not have to happen but it usually does unless one is careful and zealous. The word of the Lord to the church of the Laodiceans is needed in the church across the USA. There are many rich believers and churches that are spiritually shallow but do not know it. It is rare to see a believer with a lot of money maintaining their fire for Jesus.

> *21 If you want to be perfect...sell what you have and give to the poor, and you will have treasure in heaven...23 It is hard for a rich man to enter the kingdom of heaven. (Mt. 19:21-23)*

Laodicea was a wealthy city being a center of banking, manufacturing (soft wool) and medicine. It was located by three major highways making it a wealthy city. The city was the judicial seat of the district. A famous school of medicine developed treatment applied to cure eye diseases. Its great weakness was in lacking a water supply. An aqueduct brought them water from neighboring Hierapolis (known for its hot springs) and Colossae (known for its cold springs).

Jesus' Revelation of Himself

> *14 These things says the Amen, the Faithful and True Witness, the Beginning of the creation of God...(Rev. 3:14)*

This description reveals aspects of Jesus' personality and ministry. It emphasizes His tender care for our lives and His intervention to help us walk closely with Him and to receive His promises. **The Amen** – means to "be true or established". Jesus is the Amen because His promises are certain and sure. Twenty five times John used the word, amen (Greek "amhn"). It is translated as, "truly, truly, I say to you". The "God of truth" (Isa. 65:17), is literally "the God of Amen". Amen was pronounced when one agreed with the promises and consequences of an oath (Num. 5:22; Deut. 27:15ff.; Neh. 5:13; Jer. 11:5). Being the Amen, Jesus lived in perfect agreement with His Father. As the head of the church, He requires that we agree with Him to release the certainty of His blessings. We have to relate to Jesus on His terms. We must do it His way. Jesus is the one who agrees with God and requires that we agree with Him to release His purposes. All of the promises of God are yes and amen. All the promises of God are yes because they are true. They are "amen" because we must agree with them. God's promises for increased blessing are invitations to partnership not unconditional guarantees.

> *20 For all the promises of God in Him are Yes, and in Him Amen... (2 Cor. 1:20)*

The Faithful and True Witness – what He speaks is reliable and truthful (Rev. 3:7). He was about to tell them the truth in both positive and negative ways. He revealed such great promises in Rev. 3:18-21 along with negative truths about their spiritual problems in Rev. 3:17-18. He does not ever exaggerate or flatter. Most only preach and prophesy of positive things.

The beginning of the creation of God – He is the beginning or "first" in cause (source) and authority. The power and authority of creation "begins" with Him (Jn. 1:3; Col. 1:16-17; Rev. 1:8; 21:6). He is the uncreated God like the Father and the Spirit. There was never a time they did not exist. This was meant to arouse the Laodiceans into zealous repentance instead of being so impressed with their financial prosperity. The creator of the earth was speaking to them.

Correction for Compromise

> *15 I know your works, that you are neither cold nor hot. I could wish you were cold or hot. 16 So then, because you are lukewarm, and neither cold nor hot, I will vomit you out of My mouth. 17 Because you say, 'I am rich, have become wealthy, and have*

> *need of nothing'--and do not know that you are wretched, miserable, poor, blind, and naked... (Rev. 3:15-17)*

You are neither cold nor hot. I could wish you were cold or hot – the spiritually cold are in a better position to see their great need. At least they know they are in trouble. They are easier to convert. When a person feels the emptiness of a cold heart he searches for answers.

Because you are lukewarm, and neither cold nor hot, I will vomit you out of My mouth – the Greek word (emew) is "to vomit". He loves them and has not lost interest in them (v. 19). Jesus' heart was sick (or His stomach hurt) with concern about them and what they are losing in their relationship with Him. Jesus knows all the lost eternal opportunities they are missing out on. Jesus quoted the warning of judgment seen in Lev. 18. The land of Israel was said to "vomit the people out" of the land in judgment.

> *25 For the land is defiled; therefore I visit the punishment of its iniquity upon it, and the land vomits out its inhabitants. 26 You shall therefore keep My statutes...28 lest the land vomit you out also when you defile it, as it vomited out the nations that were before you. (Lev. 18:25-28)*

You say, 'I am rich and have become wealthy' – they claimed God's financial blessing but it turned out to injure their heart.

You say, 'I have need of nothing' – instead of being desperate for more. I have need of nothing expresses their spiritual complacency.

Many wish they were more on fire for Jesus but they decide to wait until later to make zealous changes. They were too proud to

The Church without Spot or Wrinkle

clearly see their true condition. They were intoxicated with their financial blessing. Self satisfaction is often promoted by financial abundance with its power and comfort.

What we gain in God today *(heart reality and ministry impact)* is often lost tomorrow. Over the years, one may develop a larger profile with greater influence yet their heart reality is less than it was ten years previously. Our lifestyle decisions declare how we feel about our spiritual condition. Most say, "I need more of Jesus". The way we spend our time and money is proof of how desperate we are.

You do not know that you are wretched, miserable, poor, blind, and naked – this is one of the most disturbing things that Jesus can say to a born again believer.

Wretched – this from the Greek words that mean "calloused and hardened." They were calloused and spiritually dull.

Miserable – spiritual sickness result in loss of appetite for the Word and prayer. Believers in the "spiritual ICU" have no spiritual appetite. Hunger is a sign of recovery.

Poor – being spiritually deficient is opposite of being "poor in spirit" (Mt. 5:3). Many believers have nothing in their eternal bank account. How much is in yours?

Blind – spiritual blindness means to lack revelation of God and one's spiritual condition.

Naked – without garments in the age-to-come that express their love for Jesus in this age.

Exhortation to Respond: Buy Gold and Garments and Use Eye Salve

> *18. I counsel you to buy from Me gold refined in the fire, that you may be rich; and white garments, that you may be clothed, that the shame of your nakedness may not be revealed; and anoint your eyes with eye salve, that you may see. 19 As many as I love, I rebuke and chasten. Therefore be zealous and repent. (Rev. 3:18-19)*

Jesus gave three exhortations with promises that each carry temporal and eternal applications. He was not speaking to believers about receiving salvation but a new quality in their walk with God. **Buy from Me gold refined in the fire, that you may be rich** – the gold of godly character makes us rich in this age by tenderizing our heart to feel more of God's love and enlarging our desire for Him and for righteousness.

> *7 That the genuineness of your faith, being much more precious than gold...though it is tested by fire, may be found to praise, honor, and glory at the revelation of Jesus... (1 Pet. 1:7) 12 Beloved, do not think it strange concerning the fiery trial which is to try you, as though some strange thing happened to you... (1 Pet. 4:12)*

Purified gold does not come easy or without fire. Gold must be dug for and then put in the fire. Gold refined by fire involves a costly and painful process to remove the dross.

> *2 Who can endure the day of His coming? And who can stand when He appears? For He is like a refiner's fire and like launderer's soap. 3 He will sit*

> *as a refiner and a purifier of silver; He will purify the*
> *sons of Levi, and purge them as gold and silver,*
> *that they may offer to the LORD an offering in*
> *righteousness. (Mal. 3:1-3)*

Acquiring gold with its richness refers to more than what is in our heart in this age. It also speaks of eternal gold or treasure that will be seen in the heavenly mansions, crowns, garments, etc. Gold is only one facet of our eternal reward but it is a real one. This eternal gold is given according to the measure of our love and obedience. *I counsel you to buy white garments, that you may be clothed, that the shame of your nakedness may not be revealed –* righteous living results in the reward of eternal garments. Our garments begin with the gift of righteousness that is imputed to us by faith (2 Cor. 5:21). However, here Jesus is speaking of experiential righteousness or acts of righteousness.

> *8 To her it was granted to be arrayed in fine linen,*
> *clean and bright, for the fine linen is the righteous*
> *acts of the saints. (Rev. 19:8)*

To be naked or shamed in eternity is to be devoid of the reward of heavenly garments. All believers have the robe of righteousness, yet Jesus warns us of the shame of nakedness or "lacking the reward of added clothing" that reveals one's commitment to Jesus in this age. To receive the reward of clothing as a statement of honor is what Joseph received from Pharaoh (Gen 41:42) and Mordecai received from King Ahasuerus (Esth. 6:6-11).

> *15 Blessed is he who watches, and keeps his*
> *garments, lest he walk naked and they see his*
> *shame. (Rev. 16:15) 4 You have a few...who have*
> *not defiled their garments; and they shall walk with*
> *Me in white, for they are worthy. 5 He who*
> *overcomes shall be clothed in white garments...*

(Rev. 3:4-5) 28 Abide in Him, that when He appears, we may have confidence and not be ashamed before Him at His coming. (1 Jn. 2:28).

Anoint your eyes with eye salve that you may see – people put eye medicine (eye salve) on their eyes in seeking to be cured of eye disease. Laodicea's famous medical school exported a "powder" used as an eye salve. This Phrygian powder was applied to the eyes as doughy paste. Jesus was saying that we must take action to cure our spiritually sick eyes. Only the Holy Spirit can give us revelation of Jesus and His Word. However, we can take natural steps as we take time to feed on the Word and turn our eyes away from worthless things that dull our spirit. **I counsel you to buy from Me** – Jesus exhorts us to "buy gold" or to engage in the God ordained process of acquiring a deep relationship with God. In buying gold or garments, we do not earn them but we "invest ourselves in a costly way" to position ourselves to receive them. "Buy" is from Isa. 55:1-3. No one can literally buy anything from God.

Prayer of Repentance from Being Lukewarm

<u>The Church of Laodicea</u> - We repent from being made lukewarm (through false and perverted doctrines of prosperity.) <u>Lord, we commit to give our hearts to you as a living sacrifice, and make a vow to you to offer our money to you for the building of your house of prayer, and cities of refuge throughout this nation and world.</u>

Without Spot or Wrinkle

In order for God's house to become a house of prayer we're going to have to become a House of purity. Jesus, once again, is going to have to cleanse the church from corrupt systems she's relied on and allowed to operate within the 21st century church. In the last days, Jesus is going to release to his church a hearing ear like no other time in church history, so that he that hath an ear to hear will be able to hear what the Spirit is saying to His church. It's through this hearing ear of the prophetic that the church will be cleansed as a pure bride without spot wrinkle or any such thing.

CHAPTER 10

PREPARING FOR THE DAY OF THE LORD

Day of the Lord: The 2 Extremes Related To Jesus' Return

11 For the day of the LORD is great and very terrible; who can endure it? (Joel 2:11)

At the end of the age God is raising up Forerunner ministers in the context of night & prayer. These Ministers are being positioned to prepare the Church for the coming day of the Lord. God has used men like Mike Bickle and the IHOP leadership team to bring revelation on the unique dynamics of the day of the Lord. This Chapter is dedicated to what that day is, and the message end-time forerunners will release in preparation for that day.

The Day of the Lord refers to the unusual events (positive and negative) that will escalate dramatically in the 3½ years just before Jesus returns. The 2-fold nature of this time is seen in the great blessing it releases on those who call on Jesus and the judgment for those who refuse Him.

The prophets asked, "Who can endure the Day of the Lord events?" Who can experience God's favor, deliverance and power in this unique time? Forerunners will have the answer to this.

What Is The Forerunner Message?

Forerunners prepare the way by preparing people to prepare the nations for Jesus' return.

> 3 *The voice of one crying in the wilderness: "Prepare the way of the LORD; make straight in the desert a highway for our God...5 The glory of the LORD shall be revealed and all flesh shall see it together (at Jesus' Second Coming)... (Isa. 40:3-5) 10 Prepare the way for the people; build up the highway! Take out the stones, lift up a banner for the peoples! 11 Say..., "Surely your salvation is coming..." (Isa. 62:10-11)*

In Isa. 40:3, forerunners prepare a highway "for God" whereas in Isa. 62:10 they prepare the highway "for the people". It is one highway seen from two points of view. Forerunners represent God and His interests in Isa. 40, whereas in Isa. 62, the intercessors represent the people. The highway God walks on is the voluntary agreement of His people as they partner with Him. Forerunners are messengers who proclaim "now" what the Holy Spirit is "soon" to emphasize in a universal way across the nations. They are "one short step" ahead of what the Holy Spirit is about to openly release, so they can *prepare the people to respond rightly to Jesus* by making known God's plans so the people can make sense of what will happen before it actually happens. Forerunners bring new understanding or paradigms of God and His End-Time activity and plans.

Seven Theological Premises of the Forerunner Ministry

Forerunners are "messengers" who function with a specific message in different spheres of life.

Premise #1: There will be *"unique dynamics"* in the generation the Lord returns. It will witness the *greatest demonstration of power* both God's and Satan's (Rev. 13). The three "supernatural generations" in Scripture are the generation of Moses (Ex. 7-10), the generation of the apostles, and the generation Jesus returns in which the miracles done by Moses and the apostles will be combined and multiplied on a global level. It is the generation *most described* by God in His Word.

It is the generation that is *most populated*. Some estimate that there will be more people alive in this one generation in one life span (70 years) than in all history combined. After the Great Harvest, there will be more of God's people on earth than in heaven. The greatest number of people at the time of the greatest manifestation of power will require a unique preparation, focus and understanding. The unique dynamics of the generation in which history transitions to the Millennial Kingdom is the "new thing".

> 18 *Do not remember the former things, nor consider the things of old. 19 Behold, I will do a new thing, now it shall spring forth; shall you not know it? (Isa. 43:18-19)*

Premise #2: The Spirit is emphasizing the *revelation of the Father* in bringing God's family to maturity. God will raise up those who release the Father's heart in the home, church, marketplace and government (Ps 68:5-6). The Spirit is also highlighting care for the fatherless (orphans, etc.).

> 5 *I will send you Elijah the prophet before the coming of the great and dreadful day of the LORD. 6 And he will turn the hearts of the fathers to the children, and the hearts of the children to their fathers, lest I come and strike the earth with a curse. (Mal. 4:5-6)*

Premise #3: The Holy Spirit will emphasize *3 facets of the beauty of Jesus* as clearly seen in Scriptures that describe God's End-Time plans (Rev. 19; Mt. 24-25; Isa. 60-62). There will be no contradiction in Jesus' heart and ministry as He manifests His glory as a Bridegroom, King, and Judge. He does not suspend one attribute to exercise another.

1. Jesus as a *passionate Bridegroom*: has great tenderness and deep desire for His people

2. Jesus as a *powerful King*: releases power in confronting darkness and winning the lost

3. Jesus as a *righteous Judge*: upholds the standards of conduct (holiness)

Premise #4: Forerunners will participate in the *3 unprecedented activities of the Holy Spirit*:

1. *To restore the First Commandment to first place* worldwide as the Church is prepared as a worthy Bride (Mt. 22:37; Rev. 19:7).

2. *To gather the Harvest* through an unprecedented release of God's power (Rev. 7:9, 14).

3. *To release Jesus' End-Time judgments* described in Revelation (Rev. 6; 8-9; 16) *to remove everything that hinders love* in preparing the Church as a Bride. The principle of God's love in judgment is: God uses the least severe means to reach the greatest number of people at the deepest level of love without violating our free will. *To aid in gathering the Harvest* by bringing eternity to bear on the hearts of multitudes of lost humanity and by manifesting God's power. *To release God's vengeance* on those who hate Jesus and persecute His people.

God's End-Times judgment will shake 7 spheres of human life. *1) The heavens*: the sky, atmosphere, weather patterns; *2) The earth*: earthquakes, volcanoes, etc.; *3) The sea*: tidal waves, tsunamis, etc.; *4. The dry land:* vegetation and plant life; *5) All nations:* national and social infrastructures will be shaken; *6) Religious institutions:* multitudes come to Jesus as the Desire of All Nations; *7. Economic disruption:* commercial turmoil as God transfers wealth.

> 6 *I will shake heaven and earth, the sea and dry land; 7 and I will shake all nations, and theyshall come to the Desire of All Nations, and I will fill this temple with glory...8 The silver is Mine, and the gold is Mine,' says the Lord of hosts. (Hag 2:6-8)*

Premise #5: God is *preparing forerunner ministries ahead of time in the wilderness* that they may prepare others for the Day of the Lord activities. It takes a clear sense of mandate and identity as a forerunner to stay faithful long-term to grow in understanding (Dan. 11:33-35). God is raising up "friends of the Bridegroom" type forerunner ministries like John the Baptist who will fast and pray as they "stand and hear" Jesus' voice as the Bridegroom God.

> *The friend of the Bridegroom, who stands and hears him, rejoices greatly because of the Bridegroom's voice. Therefore this joy of mine (John the Baptist) is fulfilled. (Jn. 3:29)*

Premise #6: Forerunners must *live a fasted lifestyle* in the grace of God as seen in Mt. 6:1-18. This is God's way to position ourselves to tenderize our hearts to receive more revelation in faster time frames with a deeper impact on our hearts.

Premise #7: Forerunners are *best trained in context to the End-Time prayer movement*. God is raising up forerunner ministries in local congregations that are rooted in prayer that flows in the spirit of the Tabernacle of David.

Three Responses of the Church to God's End-Time Judgments

- Offense (fear, confusion, anger) will be the first reaction of believers with an un-renewed mind.

  6 *And blessed is he who is not offended because of Me. (Mt. 11:6)*

- Understanding will be given by the Holy Spirit to the End-Time Church.

  19 *Behold, a whirlwind of the LORD has gone forth in fury -- a violent whirlwind (Great Tribulation)! It will fall violently on the head of the wicked. 20 The anger of the LORD will not turn back until He has executed and performed the thoughts of His heart. In the latter days you will understand it perfectly. (Jer. 23:19-20)*

  24 *The fierce anger of the LORD will not return until He has done it, and until He has performed the intents of His heart. In the latter days you will consider it. (Jer. 30:24)*

  33 *Those of the people who understand shall instruct many… they shall fall by sword and flame, by captivity and plundering….35 Some of those of understanding shall fall(martyrdom), to refine them, purify them, and make them white, until the time of the end; because it is still for the appointed time. (Dan. 11:33-35)*

- Partnership with Jesus in intercession releases God's judgments in the way that Moses did.

  6 Let the high praises of God be in their mouth... 7 to execute vengeance on the nations, and punishments on the peoples...9 To execute on them the written judgment (written in the End-Time Scriptures)-- This honor have all His saints. (Ps. 149:6-9)

  20 Rejoice over her (judgment on End-Time Babylon), O heaven, and you holy apostles and prophets, for God has avenged you on her! (Rev. 18:20)

Becoming a Voice and Not an Echo

The Priests and Levites who were sent from the Pharisees in Jerusalem asked John who he was.

  22 Who are you...? What do you say about yourself?" 23 He said: "I am the voice of one crying in the wilderness: make straight the way of the LORD"... (Jn. 1:22-23)

The only way to understand John is to know Who He lived before. John described his heart, motivation, and forerunner ministry. He lived a *"wilderness lifestyle"* (in the Word and prayer with fasting) and then went before Jesus *"as a voice"* (not an echo) to prepare the people to receive Jesus' embrace as the Bridegroom God empowering them to walk out the first commandment as those who love God with all of their heart. We become a voice by hearing His voice and responding to it in faith and obedience. An echo only memorizes the ideas and repeats them, but a voice embodies them in the reality of their heart. There is nothing wrong with being an echo. I have echoed many truths for many years. This is how I have learned the truths. A voice speaks about things to come with clarity, power and boldness. It is a banner of hope.

Prophetic Ministry in the End-Times (Rev. 10-11)

In Rev. 10, God promises to raise up prophetic messengers (forerunners) to bring understanding that helps people avoid deception. This is an important passage for forerunner messengers. The focus of Rev. 11 is the Two Witnesses (prophets) who will preach with great power and release God's judgments against the Antichrist's systems for the final 3½ years (Tribulation).

> 3 *I will give power to my Two Witnesses, and they will prophesy 1,260 days...5 If anyone wants to harm them, fire proceeds from their mouth and devours their enemies...6 These have power to shut heaven, so that no rain falls in the days of their prophecy; and they have power over waters to turn them to blood, and to strike the earth with all plagues... (Rev. 11:3-6)*

The Two Witnesses release End-Time judgments by prophetic decrees like Moses. The plagues of Egypt are the prototype of the End-Time judgments (Exod 7-12) released by intercession (Rev. 8-9; 16). The miracles done by Elijah and Moses will be done by the Two Witnesses. This will be the Church's most glorious hour in all history! Joel prophesied of the greatest prophetic move of the Spirit in the End-Times on all nations that would occur before the Day of the Lord or Jesus' Coming (Joel 2:28-32; Acts 2:17-21; Eph. 4:11-13; Rev. 11:10, 18; 16:6;18:20, 24). This outpouring of the Spirit will be manifest in many ways on national and regional levels. All God's praying people will receive dreams and visions.

> 28 *I will pour out My Spirit on all flesh; your sons and your daughters shall prophesy...29 On My menservants and on My maidservants I will pour out My Spirit...30 I will show wonders in the heavens and in the earth: blood and fire and smoke...31 before the coming of the great and awesome day of the Lord...32 whoever calls on the name of the Lord shall be saved. (Joel 2:28-32)*

The Lord released a down payment of Joel's prophecy on the day of Pentecost (Acts 2:16). It was not completely fulfilled in Peter's generation. For example, the sun and moon did not grow dark with signs including blood, fire and smoke. The Spirit in Acts 2 only rested on 120 believers in one city, Jerusalem. The fullness of this prophecy requires a global dimension. The glory of the Angel (Rev. 10:1-3): the forerunner anointing

> 1 *I saw another mighty angel...clothed with a cloud. A rainbow was on his head, his face was like the sun, and his feet like pillars of fire. 2 He had a little book open in his hand. He set his right foot on the sea and left foot on the land 3 and cried...as when a lion roars. (Rev. 10:1-3)*

The angel's authority prophetically pictures aspects of the glory released on God's messengers.

1. Mighty angel: forerunners will operate in the power of the Holy Spirit.

2. Robed in a cloud of glory: forerunners will experience God's Shekinah glory.

3. Rainbow around his head: forerunners will emphasize God's promises and mercy.

4. Face shines like the sun: forerunners will receive God's might in their inner man (Eph. 3:17).

5. Feet are like pillars of fire: forerunners will release God's holy judgment to establish love.

6. Feet on the sea and land: forerunners will take possession of their inheritance across the earth.

7. Cries out like a roaring lion: forerunners will pray and prophesy in the boldness of a lion. End-Time forerunner messengers: the seven thunders prophets

> *2 He (angel) had a little book open in his hand. He set his right foot on the sea and his left foot on the land…3 When he cried out, seven thunders uttered their voices (messages). 4 When the seven thunders uttered their voices, I was about to write; but I heard a voice…saying, "Seal up the things which the seven thunders uttered, and do not write them." (Rev. 10:2-4)*

A prophetic book being "open" indicates that its contents are knowable. The angel probably read its contents to John. This may be the same book with the same prophetic information that Daniel received. Daniel 10-12 is a parallel passage with Rev. 10-13. Daniel sealed up similar prophetic information with an angel of similar glory (Dan. 12:4-10).

> *4 Daniel…seal the book until the time of the end…9 For the words are closed up and sealed till the time of the end… (Dan. 12:4-9)*

John was told to seal the seven thunder prophetic messages until the End-Times. This was similar to what happened to Daniel. For a book to be opened implies that its prophetic information was made known in a widespread way. For a book to be sealed implies its info is not to be made known. The angel's open book was probably the book Daniel sealed (Dan. 12:4). Many think its contents were what John wrote about in Rev. 11-22 and prophesied to the nations (v. 11). The little book the angel opened was a different set of prophecies uttered from by the seven thunders voices.

The Mandatory Preparation for the End-Time Messengers

8 Go, take the little book which is open in the hand of the angel...9 I went to the angel and said, "Give me the little book." He said, "Take and eat it; and it will make your stomach bitter, but it will be as sweet as honey in your mouth." 10 I took the little book out of the angel's hand and ate it, and it was as sweet as honey in my mouth. When I had eaten it, my stomach became bitter. 11 And he said to me, "You must prophesy again about many peoples, nations, tongues, and kings." (Rev. 10:8-11)

John eating the scroll as Ezekiel did (Ezek. 2:10-3:3) is a prototype for End-Time messengers. The principle being taught is that we must take time to digest God's revelation of the End-Times. John sees the book open and "eats it" then makes it known. John saw and prophesied about the Beast (Rev. 11-13). This was, in essence, what Daniel prophesied about in Dan. 7-12. Daniel and John had unusual revelation and devotion to the Word from their youth. They both had visitations when older. Daniel modeled fasting, praying and studying (Dan. 9:20-22; 10:1-13).

1 Son of man...eat this scroll, and go, speak to the

> *house of Israel." 2 So I opened my mouth, and He caused me to eat that scroll. 3 He said, "Son of man, feed...and fill your stomach with this scroll..." 4 He said, "Go to Israel and speak with My words to them. (Ezek. 3:1-4)*

Sweet: message of victory, salvation and justice with deliverance to the oppressed worldwide. Bitter: message of judgment worldwide that brings persecution to the messengers (Lk. 19:41). *John must prophesy* because God only releases the fullness of His purposes as His people pray and prophesy their release under the leadership of the Holy Spirit.

CHAPTER 11

THE REVELATION OF JESUS CHRIST: *Bridegroom, King and Judge* (Rev. 1)

The message of the book of revelation is the majesty of Jesus. The main theme of the book of revelation is to reveal the personality, power and action plan of Jesus in preparing his church to participate with him in releasing God's glory in all the nations.

> *¹ The <u>Revelation of Jesus Christ</u>, which God gave Him to show His servants... (Rev. 1:1)*

The Father commissioned Jesus to reveal more of His majesty to His Church. Jesus revealed Himself as the Bridegroom King who judges all that hinders love as He takes over the earth. Jesus is a passionate Bridegroom who is filled with tender yet jealous love. Jesus will come only in context to a prepared Bride who lives in unity with Him and the Spirit.

> *⁷ The marriage of the Lamb has come...His wife has <u>made herself ready</u>. (Rev. 19:7)*

Jesus is a King who will intervene to save the earth by taking over the government of every nation for the glory of God and the good of His people forever. Jesus will replace all the unrighteous governments on earth with righteous leaders and laws.

> *¹⁵ The seventh angel sounded...voices in heaven, saying, "The <u>kingdoms of this world have become the kingdoms of our Lord</u>...and He shall reign forever!" (Rev. 11:15)*

Jesus is a righteous and wise Judge, who works redemptively to confront hatred of God and truth in order to establish love across the whole earth (Rev. 16:5-7; 19:1-5).

> ³ <u>Great</u> and <u>marvelous</u> are Your (Jesus) works...<u>just</u> and <u>true</u> are Your ways, O King of the saints! 4...For Your <u>judgments</u> have been manifested. (Rev. 15:3-4)

The nations will hate Jesus and rage with anger against His love and truth (Ps. 2:1-3).

> ¹⁸ The nations were <u>angry</u> and Your wrath has come... (Rev. 11:18)

There is no contradiction between Jesus as Bridegroom and Judge. Jesus has burning love and fierce zeal to remove everything that hinders love. His love is expressed and promoted by His redemptive judgments to remove all that hinders love by confronting those who aggressively oppose and hate His love and leadership. The zealous Jesus of Armageddon who slays the wicked is the same Bridegroom God of love and tenderness.

We marvel and tremble in seeing what His love is capable of and how far it will go. So fierce is His zeal for love that He became human and was crushed by the wrath of God. This is the same love, zeal and wisdom that He manifests in killing multitudes who hate God at Armageddon. He uses the <u>least severe</u> means to reach the <u>greatest number</u> of people at the <u>deepest level</u> of love.

The theme of this book is Jesus returning to take leadership of the earth in deep partnership with His people

> ⁷ Behold, <u>He is coming with clouds</u>, and every eye will see Him... (Rev. 1:7)

Daniel prophesied that the Messiah as the Son of Man (God-Man) would rule all the nations.

> ⁹ The Ancient of Days (the Father)...His garment was white as snow, and the hair of His head was like pure wool...13 Behold, One like the <u>Son of Man</u>,

> *coming with the <u>clouds</u> of heaven! He came to the Ancient of Days...14 To Him was given dominion and glory and a kingdom, that <u>all peoples</u>...should serve Him...27 Then the...the greatness of the kingdoms under the whole heaven, <u>shall be given to the people</u>, the saints of the Most High. (Dan. 7:9-14, 27)*

As King of Kings, Jesus will strike the nations to remove their unrighteous leaders and laws.

> [15] *He should <u>strike the nations</u>...He Himself treads...the <u>fierceness and wrath of God</u>. 16 He has on His robe...a name written: King of kings and Lord of lords. (Rev. 19:15-16)*

Jesus is preparing His Church to operate in authority to bring a great Harvest of souls to God.

> [9] *A <u>great multitude</u>...of <u>all nations</u>...and tongues standing before the Throne... (Rev. 7:9)*

> [14] *This gospel...will be preached in <u>all the world</u>...and <u>then the end will come</u>. (Mt. 24:14)*

The Biblical View of the Great Tribulation

The primary theme of the Tribulation is <u>God's judgment against the Antichrist's empire that is being released by the End-Time Church under Jesus' leadership</u>. The secondary theme is tribulation against the saints from the Antichrist (Rev. 12:12; 13:4, 8). In the Book of Acts, some were martyred, yet its primary theme was the acts of the Spirit through the praying apostles.

We need not fear the Tribulation as powerless victims seeking to escape it. We stand boldly as Jesus' Bride who releases its' judgments under His leadership. Moses did not seek to escape his role in releasing tribulation on Pharaoh nor did the apostles seek to avoid their role in the Book of Acts. The Church is not absent for the Tribulation but under Jesus' leadership will release the Tribulation by prayer. Jesus will not release it without the partnership of His praying Bride.

The Book of Revelation: End-Time Book of Acts

Book of Revelation is the *End-Time Book of Acts* given to us in advance so we may walk in a unified prayer focus by knowing the sequences of the Seals and Trumpets. We will engage in the prayer of faith globally to bind and loose according to God's will (Mt. 16:18-19; 18:18-19).

> *18 On this rock I will build My church, and the gates of Hades shall not prevail against it. 19 I will give you the keys of the kingdom of heaven, and whatever you <u>bind on earth</u> will be bound in heaven, and <u>whatever you loose on earth</u> will be loosed in heaven. (Mt. 16:18-19)*

> *18 Whatever you <u>bind on earth</u> will be bound in heaven, and whatever you <u>loose on earth</u> will be loosed in heaven...19 <u>If two of you agree</u> on earth...it will be done... (Mt. 18:18-19)*

The Mt. 16 context focuses on prevailing over the authority of hell. The Mt. 18 context focuses on how the Church will function in unity (with several hundred million intercessors). As   Moses released the plagues or tribulation on Egypt and as the first apostles established the Church in the Book of Acts, so the Tribulation will be released by the praying Church. The Book of Revelation is a record of the acts of the Spirit through the End-

Time apostles and prophets. The miracles of Exodus and Acts will be combined and multiplied on a global level. This "Jn. 14:12 prayer anointing" will loose revival and the Tribulation and will bind the works of Satan.

> [12] *The works that I do he will do also; and greater works than these he will do... (Jn. 14:12)*

The Book of Revelation is a *"canonized prayer manual"* that equips the Church to partner with Jesus in confronting Satan's authority. Jesus is coming back only after the Church is prepared in love, wisdom and faith to release the Tribulation through prayer against the Antichrist's empire. Jesus is waiting on the Church to grow up into agreement with His character and End-Time plan.

Because the Book of Revelation is canonized the entire Body of Christ will eventually use it. As Jesus' judgments progressively unfold according to their numbered sequence, the Church will become greatly unified and focused in prayer. The momentum will build as the Church sees the Seals and Trumpets unfold in numerical order. Nothing like this has ever happened in history where 100s of millions were unified with an *"infallible prayer guide"* revealing Jesus' action plan including the coming glory and pressures. If the early apostles had the Book of Acts written in advance, they would know which cities revival and/or persecution would break out.

Jesus will come ONLY in context to a praying Bride in unity with the Spirit. We cry, "Come Lord Jesus" differently after experiencing His love as the Bridegroom King.

> *The Spirit and the Bride say, "Come!" (Rev. 22:17)*

In Rev. 22:17, John records the *"final unified global prayer focus"* that crescendos after the Sixth Trumpet. All the saints will know that soon after the Sixth Trumpet is the Seventh Trumpet in which Jesus will appear in the clouds so the cry, "Come Lord Jesus" will explode worldwide. The End-Time prayer movement under Jesus' leadership will bind and release His redemptive judgments according to the will of God (Rev. 5:8; 6:9-11; 8:3-5; 9:13; 10:6; 14:18; 16:7; 19:2).

> [4] *The prayers of the saints, ascended before God...5 Then the angel took the censer, filled it with fire from the altar, and threw it to the earth... (Rev. 8:4-5)*

As a warrior, John prayed out of his anger and pride for fire to fall on a city instead of praying out of bridal partnership with Jesus who only always works to establish love.

> [54] *Lord, do You want us to command fire to come down from heaven and consume them...? 55 He rebuked them, and said, "You do not know what manner of spirit you are of". (Lk. 9:54-55)*

The spirit of prophecy and prayer is to make known the testimony of Jesus or what is on His heart. Revelation was given to equip the Church to operate in the spirit of prophecy and prayer.

> [10] *For the testimony of Jesus is the spirit of prophecy. 11 Now I saw heaven opened, and behold, a white horse. He who sat on him...He judges and makes war. (Rev. 19:10-11)*

Revelation changed my paradigm of the prayer and prophetic movement, which is currently very sincere and dear to God. However, it is profoundly deficient on what the Book of Revelation teaches about the most significant generation in history. Jesus allowed the Devil to see His End-Time plan by publishing this "canonized prayer guide". *Satan's schemes* are same as those he has used through history because they are effective. First, he causes some in the Church to <u>reduce Revelation to allegorical poetry</u>, thus, causing the Church to be *indifferent* to Jesus' perfect End-Time action plan.

Second, he causes some to misinterpret Revelation either by the <u>pre-tribulation Rapture</u> so they fix their hope on *escaping* it or by a <u>defeatist view</u> so they *retreat in fear*.

Third, he causes some to present Jesus' judgments as a <u>demonic contradiction</u> to love so they end up *offended* as this aspect of Jesus' majesty. This is the "role reversal" scheme that he used in the Garden of Eden in convincing Adam that God's work was demonic.

Satan wants the Church to be in confusion about Jesus' judgments to *divide* the Church about His loving leadership, to keep the Church *unprepared* in prayer and to eventually be *offended* at Jesus when His judgments surely come to pass instead of trusting in His loving leadership. All heaven will rejoice as Jesus releases judgment against those who hate God and His salvation (Rev. 11:17-18; 15:3-4; 18:20-21; Ps. 82:8; 94:1-17).

> [1] *A great multitude in heaven, saying, "<u>Alleluia</u>...2 For <u>true and righteous are His judgments</u>, because He has judged the great harlot..." 3 Again they said, "<u>Alleluia</u>!" (Rev. 19:1-3)*

The Scripture defines false prophets as those who promise peace in a time of impending judgment (Jer. 23:16-22; Ezek. 13:10; Zeph. 1:12). In the End-Times there will be a battle for the truth about Jesus. The Holy Spirit was sent to glorify and exalt Jesus by guiding us into all truth about Him (Jn. 16:13-14). In the End-Times some believers will give heed to doctrines that lie about the person of Jesus.

> [1] *The Spirit <u>expressly says</u> that in <u>latter times</u> some will depart from the faith, <u>giving heed</u> to deceiving spirits and doctrines of demons...2 having their conscience seared... (1 Tim. 4:1-2)*

The conflict in the End-Times will center around defining who Jesus is. Three truths about Jesus that offend humanists include, first, His deity thus His right to establish absolute standards for which the nations are accountable to Him for. Jesus is NOT tolerant and accepting of everyone's view of righteousness and love. Second, the only way of salvation is through Jesus. Third, that He possesses the wisdom and love to judge sin in time and eternity.

> [22] *Consider the <u>goodness</u> and <u>severity</u> of God: on those who fell, severity; but toward you, goodness, if you continue in His goodness. Otherwise you also will be cut off. (Rom. 11:22)*

CHAPTER 12

THE CHURCH IN THE BOOK OF THE REVELATION

They overcame him (Satan) by the blood of the Lamb and by the word of their testimony, and they did not love their lives to the death. (Rev. 12:11)

Those in the Church that teach a pre-tribulation rapture teach that the church will be raptured before the events that begin in Revelation 4:1. This teaching is based on the argument that since the term *Church* is not used in chapters 4–21 of Revelation, the Church must no longer be on earth at that time. However, this assumption is based on silence rather than on Scripture. I shared in chapter 7 how this assumption is based on faulty presuppositions rather than concrete evidence. There is much evidence in Revelation that the saints are living and functioning on earth during the tribulation. The great harvest of souls from all nations occurs during the tribulation. The Church will not be absent at the time of our greatest increase and effectiveness in evangelism.

> *Behold, a great multitude which no one could number, of all nations, tribes, peoples, and tongues, standing before the throne...14 These are the ones who come out of the great tribulation, and washed their robes and made them white in the blood of the Lamb. (Rev. 7:9,14) This gospel of the kingdom will be preached in all the world as a witness to all the nations, and then the end will come. (Matt. 24:14)*

Below are some scriptural facts about the end-time church and our place and position in the book of the Revelation.

- The saints will overcome Satan and the Antichrist with great victory during the tribulation.

> *They overcame him (Satan) by the blood of the Lamb and by the word of their testimony, and they did not love their lives to the death. (Rev. 12:11) I saw...those who have the victory over the beast (Antichrist), over his image and over his mark...standing on the sea of glass, having harps of God. (Rev. 15:2)*

- Some saints will be martyred during the tribulation. The Church must be on earth at that time.

> *For they have shed the blood of saints and prophets... (Rev. 16:6)I saw the woman (Harlot Babylon), drunk with the blood of the saints and with the blood of the martyrs of Jesus. (Rev. 17:6)*
>
> *In her (Harlot Babylon) was found the blood of prophets and saints... (Rev. 18:24)*
>
> *He has avenged on her (Harlot Babylon) the blood of His servants shed by her. (Rev. 19:2)Rejoice...you holy apostles and prophets, for God has avenged you on her! (Rev. 18:20)*
>
> *How long...until You judge and avenge our blood on those who dwell on the earth? 11...they should rest a little while longer, until both the number of their fellow servants and their brethren, who would be killed as they were, was completed. (Rev. 6:10–11)*
>
> *I saw the souls of those who had been beheaded for their witness to Jesus and for the word of God, who*

> had not worshiped the beast (Antichrist)... (Rev. 20:4)

- Satan and the Antichrist will war against the saints during the tribulation.

> *The dragon (Satan) was enraged with the woman, and he went to make war with the rest of her offspring, who keep the commandments of God and have the testimony of Jesus Christ. (Rev. 12:17)*

> *It was granted to him (Antichrist) to make war with the saints...10 Here is the patience and the faith of the saints. (Rev. 13:7, 10) Here is the patience of the saints; here are those who keep the commandments of God and the faith of Jesus. 13...Blessed are the dead who die in the Lord from now on. (Rev. 14:12–13)*

- The 144,000 Jewish servants of God are followers of Jesus.

> *Do not harm the earth, the sea, or the trees till we have sealed the servants of our God on their foreheads...4 One hundred and forty-four thousand of all the tribes of the children of Israel were sealed... (Rev. 7:3–4)*

> *One hundred and forty-four thousand, having His Father's name written on their foreheads...3 were redeemed from the earth. 4 These...follow the Lamb wherever He goes. These were redeemed from among men, being first fruits to God and to the Lamb. (Rev. 14:1–4)*

> *They were commanded not to harm the grass of the earth, or any green thing, or any tree, but only those men who do not have the seal of God on their foreheads. (Rev. 9:4)*

- The saints' prayers during the tribulation will release the trumpet judgments.

  > *Another angel…was given much incense, that he should offer it with the prayers of all the saints…4 The smoke of the incense, with the prayers of the saints, ascended before God from the angel's hand. 5 Then the angel took the censer, filled it with fire from the altar, and threw it to the earth. (Rev. 8:3–5)*

- Jesus comes back to earth in answer to the prayer of saints crying out for His return.

  > *The Spirit and the Bride say, "Come!" (Rev. 22:17)*

- Prophetic ministry will increase greatly during the tribulation (Rev. 11:3–6, 10, 18; 16:6; 18:20, 24; 22:6–9; Joel 2:28–32; Acts 2:17–21; Eph. 4:13; Dan. 11:33–35; 12:10). The seven thunders prophecies were sealed in John's generation with the intention of being released during the tribulation to the end-time prophets.

  > *When the seven thunders uttered their voices, I was about to write; but I heard a voice from heaven saying to me, "Seal up the things which the seven thunders uttered, and do not write them." (Rev. 10:4)*

- The two witnesses or prophets will be born-again believers.

  > *I will give power to my two witnesses, and they will prophesy 1,260 days… (Rev. 11:3) These two prophets tormented those who dwell on the earth. (Rev. 11:10)*

148

Calculating the number of the Antichrist will only be relevant to those living in the tribulation.

> *Here is wisdom. Let him who has understanding calculate the number of the beast, for it is the number of a man: His number is 666. (Rev. 13:18)*

- Believers who watch and pray until the time of the bowl judgments (Rev. 16) will be blessed instead of suffering loss at the time of Jesus' Second Coming.

> *Behold, I am coming as a thief. Blessed is he who watches, and keeps his garments, lest he walk naked and they see his shame." (Rev. 16:15)*

- Only those on earth during the events prophesied by John are in a position to keep the prophecy.

> *Behold, I am coming quickly! Blessed is he who keeps the words of the prophecy of this book." (Rev. 22:7)*

- An angel commands God's people to leave Babylon just prior to her final judgment in Rev. 18.

> *I heard another voice from heaven saying, "Come out of her, my people, lest you share in her sins, and lest you receive of her plagues. (Rev. 18:4)*

- Jesus' bride is prepared in the context of the final judgment of Babylon during the tribulation (Rev. 19:1-10). An angel revealed to Daniel that the saints would be purified during the pressures of the tribulation (Dan. 11:33–35; 12:10)

> *For the marriage of the Lamb has come, and His*

wife has made herself ready. 8 And to her it was granted to be arrayed in fine linen, clean and bright, for the fine linen is the righteous acts of the saints. (Rev. 19:7)

Many shall be purified, made white, and refined, but the wicked shall do wickedly...but the wise shall understand. (Dan. 12:10)

CHAPTER 13

THE ROLE OF PRAYER IN THE BOOK OF THE REVELATION & THE END-TIME CHURCH

The role of prayer of the Church in the book of the revelation will release power, signs & wonders in the earth that will be like that seen on Moses and Elijah. We will have the spirit of confrontation to deal with sin, sickness, evil and an ungodly church and political system that will be challenged by the end time prayer movement. As they were in the prayer movements seen both in Moses' day in Egypt and in Elijah's day in Israel, the end-time church is going to have power to confront sin and Satan himself. As Elijah on Mt Carmel, challenging the ungodly, wicked, religious system in Israel of the prophets of Baal, and as Moses in Egypt challenging Pharaoh's system of oppression and slavery, The spirit of the prophets Moses and Elijah will come on the end-time praying church. This spirit will be for the operation of the prophetic that we will see released and raised up in the church to return His church to a House of Prayer, releasing the judgments on the religious and political systems of these last days.

This prophetic spirit of Moses and Elijah that is coming on the end-time prayer movement in His house of prayer is going be the spirit that prepares the church to confront the Anti-Christ system of the last days and stand in the face of persecution and death unflinching and unrelenting, releasing the end-time Judgments on the world recorded in the book of the Revelation and in the book of Daniel. The Church does not have this end-time spirit yet because we have not had a power encounter with the glorified Christ in prayer. Below are more scriptural facts about the end-time church and our place and position in the book of the Revelation.

- The prayers of all the saints during the tribulation will release the trumpet judgments (Rev. 8–9)

  > *Another angel...was given much incense, that he should offer it with the prayers of ALL the saints...4 The smoke of the incense, with the prayers of the saints, ascended before God...5Then the angel took the censer, filled it with fire...and threw it to the earth. (Rev. 8:3-5)*

- David prophesied about one generation that will release the judgments written in the Scripture on the nations through worship and prayer. Releasing judgment by prayer is the honor of all saints.

  > *Let the high praises of God be in their mouth...7 to execute vengeance on the nations...9 to execute on them the written judgment—this honor have ALL His saints. (Ps. 149:6–9)*

- The prayers of the martyrs in heaven will also be used to release God's end-time judgments.

  > *They cried with a loud voice, saying, "How long, O Lord, holy and true, until You judge and avenge our blood on those who dwell on the earth?" (Rev. 6:10)*

- Jesus prophesied of a generation that would release end-time judgment through 24/7 prayer.

  > *Shall God not avenge His own elect who cry out day and night to Him...? 8 I tell you that He will avenge them speedily...when the Son of Man comes, will He find faith...? (Lk. 18:7–8)*

- Jesus returns in answer to global concerts of prayer offered by the Church with a bridal identity. Every church will have a spirit of prayer in the End Times or they will cease to exist.

  The Spirit and the Bride say, "Come!" (Rev. 22:17)

- Jesus will not release the seal judgments until the bowls of prayer around the throne are full. In other words, the end-time Church will be mature in prayer BEFORE the final 3½ years.

  When He had taken the scroll...the twenty-four elders fell down before the Lamb, each having a harp, and golden bowls full of incense, which are the prayers of the saints. (Rev. 5:8)

- Through prayer, the end-time Church will bind or stop Satan's activities and loose or release Jesus' power on the Church and against the Antichrist.

  I will build My church, and the gates of Hades (Antichrist empire) shall not prevail against it. 19 I will give you the keys of the kingdom of heaven, and whatever you bind on earth will be bound in heaven, and whatever you loose on earth will be loosed in heaven. (Mt. 16:18–19)

- An angel will pray that God judges Babylon. God uses prophetic prayer to release His purposes. This includes the prayers of the saints and the prophetic intercessory decrees of angels.

  Render to her just as she rendered to you, and repay her double according to her works; in the cup which she has mixed, mix double for her. (Rev. 18:6)

- Each reference to the heavenly altar in Revelation is a reference to the End-Time prayer ministry. The altar is the place in heaven where our prayers ascend to the throne. Thus, when a judgment decree is given from the heavenly altar it is to be understood as coming as the result of prayer.

> *The sixth angel sounded: I heard a voice from the four horns of the golden altar... (Rev. 9:13) Another angel came out from the altar...and he cried with a loud cry to him who had the sharp sickle, saying, "Thrust in your sharp sickle...for her grapes are fully ripe." (Rev. 14:18) I heard another from the altar saying, "Even so, Lord God Almighty, true and righteous are Your judgments." (Rev. 16:7)*

- Isaiah prophesied of the generation that would continue in 24/7 prayer until Jerusalem was established as a praise in all the earth at the time of Jesus' Second Coming.

> *I have set watchmen (intercessors) on your walls, O Jerusalem; they shall never hold their peace day or night. You who make mention of the LORD, do not keep silent, 7 and give Him no rest till He establishes and till He makes Jerusalem a praise in the earth. (Isa. 62:6–7)*

- Isaiah prophesied of the generation that would worship and pray from the ends of the earth until Jesus goes forth as a mighty man of war at the time of His Second Coming.

> *Sing to the LORD a new song, and His praise from the ends of the earth...11 Let the wilderness and its cities lift up their voice...let them shout from the top of the mountains. 12 Let them give glory to the LORD, and declare His praise in the coastlands. 13*

> *The LORD shall go forth like a mighty man (Second Coming); He shall stir up His zeal like a man of war. He shall cry out, yes, shout aloud; He shall prevail against His enemies. 14 I have held My peace a long time, I have been still and restrained Myself. Now I will cry like a woman in labor, I will pant and gasp at once. 15 I will lay waste the mountains and hills... (Isa. 42:10–15)*

- Isaiah taught that the Lord will wait to hear the prayer of His people before He answers. The passage in Isaiah 30 is in the context of the generation in which the Lord returns.

> *The LORD will wait, that He may be gracious to you...19 He will be very gracious to you at the sound of your cry; when He hears it, He will answer you. (Isa. 30:18–19)*

- There is a prayer for Jesus' Second Coming offered just before His return, especially by the Messianic believers who will confess Israel's sin with identificational repentance (Isa. 64:5–13).

> *1 Oh, that You would rend the heavens! That You would come down! That the mountains might shake at Your presence...2 to make Your name known to Your adversaries, that the nations (Antichrist's armies) may tremble at Your presence (Ps. 110:5) ... (Isa. 64:1–2)*

- The Lord will answer the prayer of His people facing martyrdom at the time of His Coming.

> *He shall regard the prayer of the destitute, and shall not despise their prayer. 18 This will be written for the generation to come, that a people*

> yet to be created may praise the LORD. 19For He looked down...from heaven the LORD viewed the earth, 20 to hear the groaning of the prisoner, to release those appointed to death... (Ps. 102:17–20)

- Isaiah prophesied about the place of prayer in Egypt in the generation in which the Lord returns.

> It will be for a sign and for a witness to the LORD of hosts in the land of Egypt; for they will cry to the LORD because of the oppressors, and He will send them a Savior and a Mighty One, and He will deliver them...22 The LORD will strike Egypt, He will strike and heal it; they will return to the LORD, and He will be entreated by them and heal them. (Isa. 19:20–22)

- Isaiah prophesied about the place of prayer in chapters 24–26, along with chapters 43 and 52. Each of these passages describes the generation in which the Lord returns.

> They shall lift up their voice, they shall sing; for the majesty of the LORD they shall cry aloud from the sea. 15 Therefore glorify the LORD...in the coastlands of the sea. 16 From the ends of the earth we have heard songs: "Glory to the righteous!" (Isa. 24:14–16)

> It will be said in that day: "Behold, this is our God; we have waited (prayed) for Him...This is the LORD; we have waited for Him...and rejoice in His salvation." (Isa. 25:9)

> In the way of Your judgments, O LORD, we have waited (prayed) for You... 9 For when Your

> *judgments are in the earth, the inhabitants of the world will learn righteousness. (Isa. 26:8–9) Put Me in remembrance; let us contend together (prayer); state your case... (Isa. 43:26) Your watchmen (intercessors) shall lift up their voices, with their voices they shall sing together; for they shall see eye to eye when the LORD brings back Zion. (Isa. 52:8)*

- Jeremiah prophesied about the place of prayer in the generation in which the Lord returns.

> *Sing with gladness for Jacob, and shout among the chief of the nations; proclaim, give praise, and say, 'O LORD, save Your people, the remnant of Israel!' (Jer. 31:7) Babylon has suddenly fallen and been destroyed. Wail for her! Take balm for her pain; perhaps she may be healed. (Jer. 51:8)*

- Zechariah prophesied about the place of prayer in the generation in which the Lord returns.

> *The inhabitants of one city shall go to another, saying, "Let us continue to go and pray before the LORD, and seek the LORD of hosts..." 22 Yes, many peoples and strong nations shall come to seek the LORD of hosts in Jerusalem, and to pray before the LORD. (Zech. 8:21–22)*

> *Ask the LORD for rain in the time of the latter rain. The LORD will make flashing clouds...(Zech. 10:1) I will pour on the house of David...the Spirit of grace and supplication (Zech. 12:10) I will bring the one-third through the fire, will refine them as silver is refined...they will call on My name, and I will*

> *answer them. I will say, "This is My people"...(Zech. 13:9)*

- Joel prophesied about the place of prayer in the generation in which the Lord returns.

> *It shall come to pass that whoever calls on the name of the LORD shall be saved. For in Mount Zion and in Jerusalem there shall be deliverance... (Joel 2:32)*

Fifth Seal: The Prayer Movement Strengthened By Martyrs (Rev. 6:9-11)

> *When He [Jesus] opened the fifth seal, I saw under the altar the souls of those who had been slain for the word of God ... 10 And they cried with a loud voice, saying, "How long, O Lord, holy and true, until You judge and avenge our blood on those who dwell on the earth?" 11 Then a white robe was given to each of them; and it was said to them that they should rest a little while longer, until both the number of their fellow servants and brethren, who would be killed ... was completed. (Rev. 6:9-11)*

Jesus will release the fifth seal judgment against the Antichrist in the context of a significant increase of intercession. The prayer movement in heaven and on earth (Lk. 18:8) will increase at the fifth seal. The fifth seal judgment is against the Antichrist, not against the martyred saints. Jesus prophesied about the end-time prayer movement on earth crying out for vengeance against the great injustice of the Antichrist's reign of terror. This occurs at the time of the fifth seal.

> *Shall God not avenge [bring justice] His own elect who cry out day and night to Him, though he bears long with them? 8 I tell you that He will avenge them speedily [Tribulation]. When the Son of Man comes, will He really find faith [agreement] on the earth? (Lk. 18:7-8)*

The fifth seal judgment is more severe than the four preceding it. The judgments increase in intensity as the seals unfold. The fourth seal resulted in the death of one fourth of the earth. The first four seals were the wicked acting against each other as God removed His restraining hand. The blood of the martyrs crying out for justice in the fifth seal is powerful. It will release a new order of supernatural judgments seen in the sixth seal, followed by the trumpets and bowls. There is an acceleration of judgment after the fifth seal. It is the turning point in Revelation. The mistreatment of the righteous in the first four seals (Rev. 6:1-8) resulted in increased prayer by the saints (Rev. 6:10). The murder of the saints will stir Jesus' heart of vengeance.

> *For true and righteous are His judgments, because ... He has avenged on her the blood of His servants shed by her. (Rev. 19:2)*

Martyrdom sets into motion a domino effect in the spirit realm, which intensifies prayer. Murder backfires on the Antichrist. The shedding of the saints' blood fuels the prayer movement, purifies the Church, and releases the harvest. It will result in fearless dedication to Jesus and zeal in the prayer movement, which releases judgment. The Antichrist will be the greatest oppressor in history. God is raising up a justice movement to confront him. The end-time prayer movement is the ultimate justice movement. Jesus will confront oppressors and completely overpower them.

The wicked do not fear the prayer movement because they do not understand that the blood of martyrs fuels the prayer movement. Murder fills up the guilt of a nation.

> *You are witnesses against yourselves that you are sons of those who murdered the prophets. 32 Fill up, then, the measure of your fathers' guilt. (Mt. 23:31-32) Know certainly that your descendants will be strangers in a land [Egypt] ... and they will afflict them 400 years. 14 The nation whom they serve I will judge; afterward they shall come out with great possessions ...16 But in the fourth generation they shall return here, for the iniquity of the Amorites is not yet complete. (Gen. 15:13-16)*

The Spirit who inspires intercession in heaven in the fifth seal will inspire intercession in the Church on earth as Jesus prophesied in Luke 18:7-8. The prayer ministry in heaven gives us great insight into the prayer ministry on earth. They will mirror each other. Jesus will confront oppression to the degree that prayer ascends. The end-time prayer movement is the greatest justice movement in history. The prayers of the **saints** (Lk. 18:7-8; Isa. 42:10-16; Rev. 5:8; 22:17) join with the prayers of the **martyrs in heaven** (Rev. 6:10) and with the prayers of the **remnant of Israel** (Zech. 12:10; Isa. 64:1-12; 30:18-33; Ps. 94:1-23; 98:1-9; 99:1-9, etc.). Scripture prophesies the end-time prayer movement at the time of the fifth seal in heaven.

> *Let the high praises of God be in their mouth ... 7 To execute vengeance on the nations ... 9 To execute on them the written judgment—this honor have all His saints. (Ps. 149:6-9)*
>
> *Sing to the LORD a new song, and His praise from the ends of the earth ... 11 Let the wilderness and*

> *its cities lift up their voice ... 13 The LORD shall go forth [Jesus' coming] like a mighty man; He shall stir up His zeal like a man of war ... He shall prevail. (Isa. 42:10-13)*

> *I will pour on ... the inhabitants of Jerusalem the Spirit of grace and supplication [prayer]; then they will look on Me whom they have pierced; they will mourn for Him. (Zech. 12:10)*

> *Oh, that You would rend the heavens! That You would come down! That the mountains might shake at Your presence ... 2 to make Your name known to Your adversaries, that the nations [Antichrist's armies] may tremble at Your presence. (Isa. 64:1-2; also see Ps. 110:5)*

The prayer ministry is the governmental center of the universe. The end-time prayer movement affects the decrees in God's court by releasing favor on the saints and judgment on the wicked.

> *The horn [Antichrist] was making war against the saints, and prevailing against them, 22 until the Ancient of Days came, and a judgment was made in favor of the saints ... to possess the kingdom ... 25 He shall persecute the saints ... 26 The court shall be seated, and they shall take*
> *away his dominion ... 27 The kingdom ... shall be given to the ... saints. (Dan. 7:21-27) 9 The Ancient of Days was seated ... 10 ten thousand times ten thousand stood before Him. The court was seated ... 11 I watched till the beast was slain ... 14 to Him [Jesus] was given dominion and glory and a kingdom, that all peoples ... should serve Him. (Dan. 7:9-14)*

The Details of the Fifth Seal

Jesus opened the fifth seal: God will allow the martyrdom prophesied by Daniel to create the context for a great prayer movement. The heavenly court is in session as the saints pray. ***Under the altar:*** the golden altar of incense in heaven (Rev. 8:3-5; 9:13; 14:17-18; 16:7) is where the prayer reaches the heavenly court. In Moses' tabernacle there were two altars, the brazen altar for sacrifice and the golden altar of incense for prayer.

Until You judge and avenge our blood on those who dwell on the earth (Rev. 14:20; 16:7; 19:2,21).

To generalize this passage as referring to all the martyrs of history ignores the detail that their persecutors are still alive on earth at the time that their prayer is offered in heaven. These are martyrs killed in the end times. They pray in heaven for their persecutors, who live on the earth. "Those who dwell on the earth" refers to unbelievers in Revelation (13 times). This is a prayer to vindicate God's reputation, deliver His people, and judge the Antichrist. This is not a cry for personal revenge, but a prayer that God would remove reprobate people from oppressing others. God has no pleasure in the death of the wicked (Ezek. 33:11). We do not rejoice in judgment on individuals, but in the fact that God stops oppression. We pray for judgment only on the reprobate, who can't repent since they took the mark of the Beast.

Gods answers are seen in Revelation 6:12-17 and then followed by trumpets and bowls.

They cried, "How long": the prayer, "How long," is one of the most recorded prayers in the OT (Zech. 1:12; Ps. 6:3; 13:2; 74:10; 79:5; 80:4; 89:46; 90:13; 94:3; Dan. 8:13; 12:6-13). This is the only prayer of request in Revelation. Psalm 79 develops this vindication theme of "how long."

Lord, holy and true, until You judge and avenge our blood: Holy and *true* are emphasized in Revelation 3:7. The saints lean into sovereignty with confidence. God's judgments are holy, or pure. They always express love, justice with wisdom. They are true to God's promise to release His judgments without being too severe, nor too lenient. He judges with accurate information.

White robes: declare the saints' purity (the opposite of the guilty verdict that men gave them) and assure the saints that their prayers will be answered. They also speak of the victory. The elders (Rev. 4:4) and saints wear them (Rev. 6:11; 7:9, 13, 14; 22:14).

Rest and wait: they were not to stop crying for vengeance, but were to rest with assurance. This is in contrast to the persecution they just endured on earth (Rev. 14:8, 13). They were not to stop interceding, but to be at peace, knowing that there was a time decreed for vengeance.
Until: God's sovereign time for the fullness of judgment at the second coming will not come until the full number of martyrs is complete.

Introduction to the Sixth Seal

Jesus opened the sixth seal in answer to the prayers of the saints in the fifth seal. This seal begins a new order of supernatural judgment released by the trumpet and bowl series against the Antichrist's empire. The martyrs cried, "Avenge us" and the wicked will cry, "Hide us."

Jesus prophesied of fearful signs in the sky that point to His coming (Lk. 21:28). When He breaks the sixth seal, He will release cosmic disturbances with signs in the sky.

> *There will be signs in the sun, in the moon, and in the stars; and on the earth distress of nations ... 26 men's hearts failing them from fear and the expectation of those things which are coming on the earth, for the powers of heaven will be shaken. (Lk. 21:25-26)*

The sixth seal describes the great agitation of the universe. This is the turning point in history. *Thus says the LORD of hosts ... "I will shake heaven and earth, the sea and dry land; 7 and I will shake all nations, and they shall come to the Desire [Jesus] of all nations. (Hag. 2:6-7)*

The sixth seal is key to understanding Revelation and the outpouring of the Spirit (Joel 2:28-31).

> *I will pour out My Spirit on all flesh; your sons and your daughters shall prophesy and ... see visions ... 30 I will show wonders in the heavens and in the earth: blood and fire and pillars of smoke. 31 The sun shall be turned into darkness, and the moon into blood, before the coming of the great and awesome day of the LORD. (Joel 2:28-31)*

Our view of the sixth seal and its timing determines our view of the structure of Revelation. The Day of the Lord is both narrow and broad. The *narrow* Day of the Lord is a 24-hour day in which Jesus enters Jerusalem. The *broad* Day of the Lord starts at the Tribulation and continues until the end of the millennium as a "day" lasting 1,000 years plus 3½ years (2 Pet. 3:8). For the great day of His wrath *"has come"*—the issue is whether the Day of the Lord has just began or is it soon to follow. In the Greek, the verb *has come* can look backwards, indicating that the Day already arrived, or it can look forward as something to occur soon. The verb tenses in the hymns of Revelation are future tenses (Rev.

11:18; 19:7). Robert Thomas says the verb *elthen* ("has come") is aorist indicative, referring to a previous arrival of God's wrath.11 Robert L. Thomas, *Revelation 1-7: An Exegetical Commentary* (Chicago: Moody Publishers, 1992), 457.

The Sixfold Description of the Sixth Seal

1. *Earthquake:* is mentioned seven times in Revelation (Rev. 6:12; 8:5; 11:13 [2x], 19; 16:18 [2x]). Four times they are prophesied with the qualifying word "great" (Rev. 6:12; 11:13; 16:18 [2x]).

2. *Sun:* the darkening of the sun cannot be for a long period, or the earth would freeze. What causes this darkening? This will be Jesus' supernatural work. Yet, it could also include natural events such as volcanic eruptions that leave particles in the air as ash, dust, and debris; a nuclear fallout; or a full eclipse, which occurs when something gets in between earth and the light of the sun. The sun will be black as sackcloth. Sackcloth is the clothing of mourning and judgment (Isa.33:9). The prophets wore black and sackcloth when calling for repentance (Mt. 11:21; Lk 10:13; Rev. 11:3). The sun will one day wear the garments of death and mourning.

3. *Moon:* this will be Jesus' supernatural work. Yet it could also include natural events as gases or a lunar eclipse that change the color of the moon's light to look red. A lunar eclipse occurs during a full moon when the earth is in the way of the light of the sun. Blood red speaks of death.

4. *Stars:* asteroids and meteor showers hitting the earth. The Greek word for stars used here is *aster* from which we get the word "asteroid." An aster refers to any shining mass in the sky, including stars, comets, meteors, asteroids, or any flaming debris. The diameter of the earth is nearly 8,000

miles. Our sun is a small star that is over 800,000 miles in diameter (100 times larger than the earth). One star hitting the earth would destroy it; thus, the kings would not need to flee to the mountains. Stars will still be in the sky in the fourth trumpet (Rev. 8:12). Isaiah prophesied of stars losing their light rather than falling (Isa. 13:10). As God guided David's stone to hit Goliath, so He will guide these stones (asteroids) to destroy the Antichrist's infrastructure to stop oppressors from killing the saints and others. Meteorites will bombard the earth, as compared to a fig tree losing its figs when strong winds blow on it.

5. *Sky:* the sky will recede (split, divide, move back) as a scroll. God will cause the sky to roll back, thus opening a window to see into heaven so that worldwide leaders may witness it. *Then the sky receded as a scroll when it is rolled up, and every mountain and island was moved out of its place. (Rev. 6:14)*

6. *Mountains moved:* every mountain and island will be moved out of its place, which does not imply that they are all destroyed. No one would be able to hide in the mountains if they were all destroyed. There are five specific earthquakes prophesied in Revelation: at the sixth seal (Rev.6:12), at the release of the trumpets (Rev. 8:5), at the seventh trumpet (Rev. 11:15, 19), when the two witnesses ascend to heaven (Rev. 11:13), and at the seventh bowl (Rev. 16:17-21), which is referred to as the most severe earthquake in history (Zech. 14:4-5; Isa. 2:19; 29:6; Hag. 2:6, 7).

The Response of Unbelievers —Seven Classes

The kings of the earth, the great men, the rich men, the commanders, the mighty men, every slave and every free man, hid themselves in the caves and in the rocks of the mountains, 16 and said to the

> *mountains and rocks, "Fall on us and hide us from*
> *the face of Him who sits on the Throne and from*
> *the wrath of the Lamb! 17 For the great day of His*
> *wrath has come, and who is able to stand?" (Rev.*
> *6:15-17)*

John describes those affected from seven categories of society. He emphasizes how leaders will respond: *kings* (presidents); *great men* (world leaders); *rich men* (financial leaders); *military commanders*; *mighty men* (civil leaders); and *slaves and free men* (common class majority). Powerful world leaders are pictured as running for their lives in panic without regard for their dignity as they run to the mountains, claiming to hide from a God they said did not exist. Later in the seventh bowl, they decide to fight against Jesus (Rev. 19:17-21). Some asteroids can be detected years ahead of time so that nations will know they are coming. Unbelievers will perceive God's wrath in these signs as they cry to the mountains, "Fall on us and hide us from the wrath of the Lamb!" They run in panic, understanding the cosmic disturbances as God's judgment. We are not told how they conclude this is God's wrath. The forerunners have been proclaiming it since the opening of the first seal. This is not the second coming, because at that time, the world leaders will fight Jesus instead of running to hide from Him in the mountains (Rev. 19:17-21). The unbelievers will understand and even announce the coming of the Day of the Lord. Jesus, Peter, and Paul taught that the Day of the Lord would come as a thief, surprising many (Mt. 24:37-44; 1 Thes. 5:2-4; 2 Pet. 3:10; Rev. 3:3; 16:15).

Isaiah prophesied about people hiding in the caves (Isa. 2:10, 21, 19; Hos. 10:8; Lk. 23:30).

> *Enter into the rock, and hide in the dust, from the*
> *terror of the LORD and the glory of His majesty ...*
> *11 The haughtiness of men shall be bowed down,*

and the LORD alone shall be exalted in that day ... 19 They shall go into the holes of the rocks, and into the caves of the earth, from the terror of the Lord ... when He arises to shake the earth mightily. (Isa. 2:10-19)

The saints will see and understand in this hour in which Nahum's prophecy is fulfilled.

The mountains quake before Him, the hills melt, and the earth heaves at His presence, Yes, the world and all who dwell in it. 6 Who can stand before His indignation? And who can endure the fierceness of His anger? His fury is poured out like fire, and the rocks are thrown down by Him. 7 The LORD is good, a stronghold in the day of trouble; and He knows those who trust in Him. (Nah. 1:5-7)

Seventh Seal: Prayer Movement Strengthened By Angels
(Rev. 8:1-6)

When He opened the seventh seal, there was silence in heaven for about half an hour. 2 And I saw the seven angels who stand before God, and to them were given seven trumpets. 3 Then another angel, having a golden censer, came and stood at the altar. And he was given much incense, that he should offer it with the prayers of all the saints upon the golden altar which was before the Throne. 4 And the smoke of the incense, with the prayers of the saints, ascended before God from the angel's hand. 5 Then the angel took the censer, filled it with fire from the altar, and threw it to the earth. And there were noises, thundering, lightnings, and an earthquake. 6 So the seven angels who had the seven trumpets prepared themselves to sound. (Rev. 8:1-6)

The seventh seal judgment on the Antichrist is the strengthening of the prayer movement by angels, who offer heavenly incense as directed by the Spirit (v. 3-4) that results in fire being cast to the earth (v. 5). It is followed by seven angels preparing to sound their trumpets (Rev. 8:6).

The five specific aspects of the seventh seal include: (1) seven angels are given trumpets; (2) an angel is given heavenly incense to strengthen the prayers of the saints; (3) fire is cast to the earth; (4) cosmic disturbances occur in the sky; and (5) an earthquake occurs on earth.

Premise: the power of our prayers ultimately comes from the generosity of God's heart in desiring to answer them; the work of Jesus on the cross, which makes them acceptable; and the ministry of the Spirit on earth and in heaven throughout the entire process of our praying. Our access in prayer to the Father is given to us by the cross, the name of Jesus, and the ministry of the Holy Spirit, who apparently uses angels. Saints have a superior status to angels.

Heavenly incense: I see the heavenly incense as consisting of the intercession of Jesus and the Spirit with "much" incense offered by the angel. Together they strengthen the prayer movement. The fifth seal focuses on the prayer movement being strengthened by the prayers of the martyrs. The prayers of the saints are imperfect because of human weakness. Even so, what best helps our prayers are the intercessory prayers of Jesus and the Holy Spirit, arising as heavenly incense.

> *Christ ... at the right hand of God, who also makes intercession for us. (Rom. 8:34) Since He [Jesus] always lives to make intercession for them. (Heb. 7:25)*

> *The Spirit helps in our weaknesses. For we do not know what we should pray for ... but the Spirit Himself makes intercession for us with groanings which cannot be uttered. (Rom. 8:26) The Spirit and the Bride say, "Come!" (Rev. 22:17)*

> *I will pour on the house of David ... the Spirit of grace and supplication. (Zech. 12:10)*

The Seven Angels Commissioned With Trumpet Judgments

> *When He opened the seventh seal, there was silence in heaven for about half an hour. 2 I saw the seven angels who stand before God, and to them were given seven trumpets ... 6 The seven angels who had the seven trumpets prepared themselves to sound. (Rev. 8:1-2, 6)*

Silence in heaven: when the seven angels are given trumpets, there will be silence in heaven. There will be a dreadful yet glorious silence in heaven coming from the awful anticipation of the release of God's judgments due to seeing the seven angels. The certainty of the impending judgment causes all to be speechless. There is no adequate response for what will come. As silence fills heaven, so it will cover the earth as Jesus begins to release His final judgments.

> *The LORD is in His holy temple. Let all the earth keep silence before Him. (Hab. 2:20)*

Be silent, all flesh, before the Lord, for He is aroused from His holy habitation! (Zech. 2:13)

Be silent in the presence of the Lord GOD; for the day of the LORD is at hand. (Zeph. 1:7)

Be still, and know that I am God; I will be exalted among the nations. (Ps. 46:10)

Sound is associated with the seal judgments. The first four are released by a voice like thunder. The fifth seal describes the intercessory cry from beneath the altar. In the sixth seal, the kings cry out. Here, the terrifying silence of the seventh seal is in great contrast with the other six seals.

About half an hour: It took a priest about 30 minutes to offer incense in the temple (Lev. 16:13). *The custom of the priesthood ... to burn incense when he went into the temple of the Lord. 10 The multitude of the people was praying outside at the hour of incense. (Lk 1:9-10)*

The Fullness of the Power of Intercession

Then another angel, having a golden censer, came and stood at the altar. And he was given much incense, that he should offer it with the prayers of all the saints upon the golden altar which was before the throne. 4 And the smoke of the incense, with the prayers of the saints, ascended before God from the angel's hand. (Rev. 8:3-4)

Another angel: an eighth angel is described as being given much incense. John sees the dramatic approach of an angel with a golden censer coming to the altar and standing there. Where did the angel come from and how long did he stand at the altar?

When incense is poured out on burning coals, it produces smoke that has a sweet odor. Incense was added to the burning sacrifice by the priest in the Old Testament.

> *He shall take a censer full of burning coals of fire from the altar before the LORD, with his hands full of sweet incense ... and bring it inside the veil. 13 And he shall put the incense on the fire before the LORD, that the cloud of incense may cover the mercy seat. (Lev. 16:12-13)*

Seals, Trumpets, and Bowls: Jesus' End-Time Judgment

A coal from the heavenly altar was used by a seraph (angel) in the cleansing of Isaiah's lips.

> *One of the seraphim flew to me, having in his hand a live coal which he had taken ... from the altar ... 7 said: "This has touched your lips; your iniquity is taken away..." (Isa. 6:6-7)*

David spoke of his prayers as coming before God as incense.

> *Let my prayer be set before You as incense. (Ps. 141:2)*

Given much incense: this angel cannot provide this incense, but it is given to him by God. Heavenly incense is connected with the prayers of saints in Revelation 5:8 showing us the importance of their "holy synergism." The role of angels in prayer is unknown.

> *The four living creatures and the twenty-four elders fell down before the Lamb, each having a harp, and golden bowls full of incense, which are the prayers of the saints. (Rev. 5:8)*

172

The angel's hand: the smoke of the incense went up with the prayers from the angel's hand to show the angel formally presenting them to God. The angelic involvement in this process signifies that God is pleased with these prayers against the Antichrist's reprobate kingdom. The angel offering the collective prayers of all the saints in God's court is the official recognition that God approves of the prayers stored up in the golden bowl (Rev. 5:8; 6:10). John, like Daniel, saw God's courtroom in His temple where judgment decrees are issued.

> *His throne was a fiery flame ... 10 ten thousand times ten thousand stood before Him. The court was seated, and the books were opened. (Dan. 7:9-10)Gather yourselves together ... 2 before the decree is issued ... before the LORD's fierce anger comes upon you ... 3 Seek the LORD, all you meek of the earth. (Zeph. 2:1-3)*

Fire Cast to the Earth

> *The angel took the censer, filled it with fire from the altar, and threw it to the earth (Rev. 8:5)*

Other angels are involved in the altar ministry of prayer and the release of fire. The most powerful force in history is the prayers of the saints in unity with God to release fire on the earth.

> *17 And another angel came out from the altar, who had power over fire. (Rev. 14:18)*

The end-of-the-age conflict will be answered by fire. Elijah said that the God who answers by fire is the true God (1 Kgs. 18:24). Even the False Prophet will call fire down from heaven. David wrote of God sending fire from His heavenly temple to kill his enemies in answer to his prayers (Ps. 18:6-14).

> *He [False Prophet] makes fire come down from heaven ... in the sight of men. (Rev. 13:13)*

Revelation 8:3-5 describes activity similar to what Ezekiel saw (Ezek. 10). He saw an angel take coals of fire from the same heavenly altar to scatter over Jerusalem. This occurred after an angel sealed the righteous in Jerusalem to protect them from judgment in Ezekiel 9:6 (Rev. 7:1-4.

> *Then He spoke to the man [angel] clothed with linen, and said, "Fill your hands with coals of fire from among the cherubim, and scatter them over the city." (Ezek 10:2)*

Fire Released By the Prayer of the End-Time Saints

Fire will be called down by the prayers of the saints through a bridal paradigm, not through an angry paradigm that prays for fire in a fleshly way. Sixty years earlier, as a young man, Jesus refused John's fleshly prayer for fire to fall on a city.

> *They entered a village of the Samaritans ... 53 But they did not receive Him ... 54 When His disciples James and John saw this, they said, "Lord, do You want us to command fire to come down from heaven and consume them, just as Elijah did?" 55 But He turned and rebuked them, and said, "You do not know what manner of spirit you are of. (Lk. 9:52-55)*

The answer to praying for judgment with a wrong spirit is to become lovesick in our preoccupation with Jesus (bridal paradigm). We pray for revival and judgment with a different spirit when it has nothing to do with our ministry but is for His glory and for justice.

God's Judgments are released by the Saints

God's judgments are not released on the saints, but by the saints. The end-time prayer movement under Jesus' leadership will release His judgments through prayer, as seen in the book of Revelation (Rev. 5:8; 6:10; 8:3-5; 9:13; 14:18; 16:7; 19:2; 22:17).

> *Let the high praises of God be in their mouth ... 7 To execute vengeance on the nations ... 9 To execute on them the written judgment—this honor have all His saints. (Ps. 149:6-9)*

As Moses released the plagues on Egypt through prayer and as the apostles released God's power through prayer in Acts, so the tribulation judgments will be released by the Praying Church. The miracles of Exodus and Acts will be combined and multiplied on a global level. *As in the days when you came out of ... Egypt, I will show them wonders. (Mic. 7:15)*

Cosmic Disturbances Including an Earthquake

> *There were noises, thundering, lightnings, and an earthquake. (Rev. 8:5)*

The seventh seal picks up where the sixth seal left off. It continues with similar cosmic disturbances, as seen in Revelation 6:12-17. The fire is followed by "noises, thundering, lightnings, and an earthquake." After the silence of Revelation 8:1, the next sounds heard are noises and peals of thunder. These manifestations are seen in Revelation (4:5; 8:5; 11:19; 16:18- 21) along with Exodus.

CHAPTER 14

THE STANDARD OF SUCCESS AND PROGRESS IN THE 21st CENTURY CHURCH – The Love Walk As Seen In the Sermon on the Mount Lifestyle and Eternal Rewards

And now abideth faith, hope, charity, these three;
but the greatest of these is charity. I Cor. 13:13

In the modern Church of the 21st century our Churches have become spotted, and full of blemishes and stains because we have made our goal in ministry and the mark of success in the church how big our church buildings are, or how many people are coming, or how many programs we have operating in our churches. If we're going to see this kingdom come of righteousness, peace and joy in the Holy Ghost, we're going to have to stop seeking ministries, and ministry success that is determined by numbers, and building sizes and we're going to have to start developing in our congregations and church memberships a seeking after our hearts growing in Love for God and for our neighbor as the barometer of success in God and ministry. In the 21st century the standard of success in the church will be our Love walk towards God and in our interpersonal relationships, the Sermon on the Mount lifestyle in our homes and neighborhoods.

The Sermon on the Mount is the constitution of God's kingdom. It is Jesus' most comprehensive statement on a believer's role in cooperating with the grace of God and is the "litmus test" to measure our spiritual development and ministry impact. In this sermon, Jesus calls His people to perfect obedience and to make this their primary goal in life. We do this by seeking to walk in all

177

the light that the Spirit gives us, realizing that pursuing obedience is not the same as attaining it.

> *48. You shall be perfect [walk in all the light you receive] as your Father...is perfect. (Mt. 5:48)*

Jesus calls us to live out the eight beatitudes (5:3-12) as we pursue 100-fold obedience (5:48). The 8 beatitudes are being poor in spirit, spiritual mourning, walking in meekness, hungering for righteousness, showing mercy, embracing purity, being a peacemaker, and enduring persecution.

> *3. Blessed are the poor in spirit, for theirs is the kingdom of heaven. 4. Blessed are those who mourn, for they shall be comforted. 5. Blessed are the meek, for they shall inherit the earth.*
>
> *Blessed are those who hunger and thirst for righteousness, for they shall be filled. 7. Blessed are the merciful, for they shall obtain mercy. 8. Blessed are the pure in heart, for they shall see God. 9Blessed are the peacemakers, for they shall be called sons of God. 10. Blessed are those who are persecuted for righteousness' sake, for theirs is the kingdom of heaven. (Mt. 5:3-10)*

Sermon on the Mount Overview:
Matthew 5 -7

In the Sermon on the Mount, Jesus calls us to live out the 8 beatitudes (5:3-12) as we pursue 100-fold obedience (5:48), as we resist 6 temptations (5:21-48), and pursue 5 kingdom activities (6:1-18) that position our hearts to freely receive more grace. We do all this with confidence in His rewards (eternal/temporal 6:19-24) and His provision (6:24-33). We do this without criticism of others who pursue God with less intensity or who oppose us (7:1-6) while we seek Jesus to intervene in our relationships (7:7-12), yet without drawing back from our wholehearted pursuit of God (7:13-14) as we discern false grace messages (7:15-20). We do all of this knowing that our obedience will be tested (7:21-27). By walking in these truths, Jesus said that we will impact society (5:13-16) and will be great in His eyes (5:19), receive treasures in heaven (6:19–20) and will live in this age with our hearts exhilarated in His grace (6:22-23).

The Beatitudes are like 8 beautiful flowers

The Beatitudes are like 8 beautiful flowers in the "garden of our heart" that God wants to fully blossom. They define love, godliness, and spiritual maturity and describe the kingdom lifestyle. Implied in all of God's commands is the promise of the enabling to walk out the command.

These 8 flowers must be cultivated as we "weed our garden" by resisting 6 temptations related to our natural lusts (5:21-48) and as we "water our garden" by pursuing 5 activities (6:1-18).

The 6 temptations are anger, immorality, disregarding the marriage covenant, making false commitments, demanding personal rights, and living with a spirit of retaliation (5:21-48).

The 5 kingdom activities are prayer, fasting, giving, serving, and blessing enemies (6:1-18). These are spiritual disciplines that position our heart before God to freely receive more grace.

179

The Eight Beatitudes: Brief Definitions (Mt. 5:3-12)

<u>*Poor in Spirit*</u> - Being poor in spirit is the foundational beatitude from which the other seven beatitudes flow. Being poor in spirit is being aware of our spiritual need to experience more of God's presence and power in our life (our heart, family, ministry, city, nation, etc.). We see the gap between what God has freely made available to us in Christ and how much we are actually experiencing.

> ³*"Blessed are the <u>poor in spirit</u>, for theirs is the kingdom of heaven." (Mt. 5:3)*

We see ourselves as spiritually poor in terms of our experience in light of the fullness of what God has made available to us in Christ. We need the Spirit's help to experience what is already ours. We see that we do not have the spiritual strength to establish godliness in our own hearts or to inspire it in others *without the Spirit's continual help* (Jn. 15:5). We have no confidence in our natural abilities to obey or serve God in the fullness of His grace without His constant help. We are not poor in spirit unless what we see moves us to seek Him more. That which Jesus' work on the cross freely <u>*worked for us*</u> is that which the Spirit progressively <u>*works in us*</u> as we seek Him.

We are to seek God earnestly that we might walk in the fullness of His grace in each season of our lives. It is by the Spirit's power that we are enabled to love God and people and to effectively inspire others to do the same. It takes more than a zealous personality, a strong mind, and a determined will to walk in fullness of grace. It requires the continual intervention of the Spirit empowering our heart, as we dialogue and engage with Him in prayer (Mt. 7:7; Jn. 15:5).

Jesus addressed this as the root problem in the "successful" church of Laodicea (Rev. 3:14-21). We must not be content with the increase in finances, popularity, impact or favor with people. Jesus wants us to repent by zealously seeking Him. The Lord told H. Pittman that the condition of the Church in the West was like the condition of the Laodiceans (see his book, *Placebo*).

> [16] *"You are* <u>lukewarm</u>... [17] *Because you say, 'I am rich,* <u>I am rich,</u> *have become wealthy, and* <u>have need of nothing'</u>— *and do not know that you are wretched, miserable, poor, blind, and naked...* [19] *As many as* <u>I love,</u> *I rebuke and chasten. Therefore be* <u>zealous</u> *and repent." (Rev. 3:16-19)*

<u>*Theirs is the kingdom*</u>: This speaks of a greater personal experience of the kingdom

<u>Mourning for breakthrough</u> ("for they shall be comforted," Mt. 5:4) Mourning refers to the pain we feel when we see the gap between what God has for us and what we are actually experiencing. We mourn seeing how little we experience as compared to how much God is willing to release to our life, ministry, and church, and to the nations. Mourning also includes the pain we feel over our sin and failure to follow through in obedience to Jesus. This beatitude is not about mourning over difficult circumstances, but rather for a greater spiritual breakthrough in light of what Jesus has made available to us.

> [4] *"Blessed are those who* <u>mourn</u>, *for they shall be comforted." (Mt. 5:4)*

Being poor in spirit speaks of how we *see ourselves*; spiritual mourning refers to how we *feel about what we see*. When we *see* differently, then we *feel* differently. The result of seeing our great need is that we feel pain as we mourn for more experience of God's presence in our life.

181

This mourning is God's gift to us; it is essential to our spiritual growth. Feeling the pain of godly desperation causes us to reorder our life to spend our strength, time, and money to seek God for all that He has made available for us.

> [10]*Godly sorrow produces repentance [renewed commitment to obey] leading to salvation [breakthrough]...*[11]*what diligence it produced in you...what indignation [against personal compromise], what fear [of god], what vehement desire [for god], what zeal. (2 cor. 7:10-11)*

Mourning and joy: We hold these two truths in tension. We rejoice in who we are in Christ and what we are experiencing in God, while we are aware of how much more there is to experience. We are grateful for all that we experience, but continually seek the Lord for a greater measure.

Shall be comforted: We will progressively experience the breakthrough of the Spirit in our lives.

Walking in meekness ("shall inherit the earth," Mt. 5:5) The meek view their resources and people and their needs from God's point of view. Jesus owns all that we possess. Our natural mindset is to see our resources (gifting, money, position, favor, etc.) as belonging to us instead of to the Lord, and to mostly use them to increase our personal comfort and honor instead of using them for the kingdom. The meek refuse to use all their resources on their own desires; instead, they use them to serve God's will and to help others.

> [5]*"Blessed are the meek, for they shall inherit the earth." (Mt. 5:5)*

Meekness also involves our indebtedness to God for all that He has given us spiritually, financially, physically, relationally, etc. Thus, the meek are filled with gratitude.

Shall inherit the earth: This promise includes influence and impact. It is partially fulfilled in this life and completely fulfilled in the age to come (Mt. 19:28; Rev. 3:21; 5:10; 20:4-6).

Hungering and thirsting for righteousness ("for they shall be filled," Mt. 5:6) Jesus exhorted us to hunger to experience more of the grace of God. He affirmed the value of seeking Him for a greater release of righteousness in our hearts, for others, and in society.

> [6] "*Blessed are those who hunger and thirst for righteousness, for they shall be filled.*" (Mt. 5:6)

Grace *increases our hunger* to earnestly press into God instead of validating spiritual passivity that does not aggressively seek God for an increase of His presence in our life. Paul pressed in for the prize of walking in the fullness of His destiny in grace. Lack of hunger is a sign of spiritual sickness. Many live in a "spiritual intensive care unit" and have no hunger for prayer or the Word. This is abnormal Christianity. Ask the Spirit for help (Mt. 7:7-11).

> [12] *Not that I have already attained...I press on, that I may lay hold of that for which Christ Jesus has also laid hold of me [fullness of Paul's destiny]...* [14] *I press toward the goal for the prize of the upward call [fullness of Paul's destiny] of God in Christ Jesus.* (Phil. 3:12-14)

Shall be filled: We will progressively experience more grace for righteousness in our lives.

Relating to others with mercy ("for they shall obtain mercy," Mt. 5:7) We are to be merciful to people who are suffering; we are to help them (Lk. 10:30-37), especially those in great need caused by poverty, sickness, oppression, persecution, or other trials. Helping others often requires denying our own comfort. We are to be merciful towards those who stumble in scandalous sins as well as to those who mistreat or complain against us.

> [7]*"Blessed are the <u>merciful</u>, for they shall obtain mercy." (Mt. 5:7)*

<u>*Shall obtain mercy*</u>: We shall receive more mercy in our circumstances from God and others.

Being pure in heart ("they shall see God," Mt. 5:8) We approach this beatitude with a deep sense of wonder and awe. Purity includes godliness in our morals, motives, and methods. There is no substitute for it for those who want to see God.

> [8]*"Blessed are the <u>pure in heart</u>, for they shall see God." (Mt. 5:8)*

<u>*Shall see God*</u>: The ultimate experience of Christianity now and for eternity is to know, or see, God (Rev. 22:4). The reality of seeing God is the highest privilege that a human being can experience. The pure will have an increased capacity to see and experience God. Purity does not "earn" revelation of God, but positions us so our spiritual capacity is enlarged to

Becoming a peacemaker ("called sons of God," Mt. 5:9) Jesus calls us to be peacemakers. This includes working to reconcile and repair relationships, individually or in society, and not creating strife in relationships by promoting ourselves. The peacemaker sees the value of investing time and energy to bring peace between individuals, families, races, and ministries, in social, civic, and marketplace issues, and even in the nations. God's peace is not sought at the expense of truth and righteousness; it is not a peace at any price.

> [9]*"Blessed are the* _peacemakers,_ *for they shall be called sons of God." (Mt. 5:9)*

Jesus warns His servants to expect persecution for being faithful witnesses of the truth. This will include being attacked physically, financially, or verbally (slandered, resisted, or ostracized).

Persecuted for righteousness sake Jesus blesses those who endure persecution and sustain their commitments to serve God in the face of resistance instead of quitting.

The _kingdom being theirs_ speaks of experiencing more of it in a personal way now (1 Pet. 4:14) and of receiving great rewards in the age to come.

> [10]*"Blessed are those who are* _persecuted for righteousness' sake,_ *for theirs is the kingdom...* [12]*Rejoice and be exceedingly glad, for* _great is your reward_ *in heaven..." (Mt 5:10–12)*

Jesus invites everyone to be great in His kingdom by walking in these Beatitudes. We cannot repent of the desire for greatness, because God designed our spirit with this longing. We are to repent for seeking it in a wrong way. God invites us to greatness without regard for outward achievements or the size of our ministry. It is based on the development of our heart in love.

185

> ¹⁹*Whoever breaks one of the least of these commandments...shall be called least in the kingdom...whoever <u>does</u> and <u>teaches</u> them, he shall be called <u>great</u> in the kingdom. (Mt. 5:19)*

Jesus invites "whoever," i.e. everyone, to be great in His kingdom by walking in these Beatitudes.

> 19*Whoever breaks one of the least of these commandments...shall be called least in the kingdom...whoever does and teaches them, he shall be called great in the kingdom. (Mt. 5:19)*

Anyone with a good eye will have a vibrant heart that is full of light. The lamp of the body, that brings light to our inner man, is the eye of our heart. "The body" means our whole person.

> 22*The lamp [source of light] of the body is the eye [of the heart]. If your eye is good, your whole body will be full of light. 23But if your eye is bad, your whole body will be full of darkness. If the light that is in you is darkness, how great is that darkness! (Mt. 6:22-23)*

Jesus ties this verse in Matt 6:22, having a good eye, with walking in these 8 flowers (beatitudes) in Matt 5. When we have our eye on these as our focus of success and greatness in this life, over material prosperity, having a big ministry, or having a big ministry impact as our goal, then our eye will be good. This is to say that our heart will be vibrant and full of light, as opposed to focusing on great ministry impact, and struggling with sin and immorality in our hearts. This is the source of our whole body being full of darkness as is recorded in Matthew 6:23, even while serving the Lord. Because our focus and goal in life and ministry is not on what Jesus considers greatness in His kingdom.

186

Our issues of sin and immorality and falling into various snares of the enemy, even as we engage in religious activities of praying and participating in significant ministry, is because we don't have these beatitudes as our standard of success and greatness in the kingdom of God.

God promises that anyone with a good eye will have a vibrant heart that is full of light and righteousness. Having a good eye means that our primary life vision is to obey and teach the 8 beatitudes—refusing the six temptations of Mt. 5:21-48 - *anger* (spirit of murder, Mt. 5:21-26), *adultery* (spirit of immorality, Mt. 5:27-30), *disregarding the sanctity of marriage* (disloyalty in relationships, Mt. 5:31-32), *false commitments* (spirit of manipulation to promote ourselves, Mt. 5:33-37), *retaliation* for personal inconveniences (spirit of revenge Mt. 5:38-42), and *inactivity* when mistreated (refusing active love, Mt. 5:43-47) – And pursuing the five kingdom activities (Mt. 6:1-20). _**serve and give**_ (charitable deeds: giving service and/or money (6:1-4,19-21), _**pray**_ (6:5-13), _**bless**_ *our adversaries* (fullness of forgiveness, 6:14-15; 5:44), and _**fast**_ (6:16-18). These are spiritual disciplines that position our heart before God to receive more grace to walk out, obey and teach the 8 beatitudes.

The lamp that brings light to our heart is the "eye of our heart" and the body is our whole person.

> [22]*the lamp [source of light] of the body is the eye [of the heart]. If your eye is* <u>*good*</u>, *your Whole body will be* <u>*full of light*</u>. [23]*but if your eye is* <u>*bad*</u>, *your whole body will be full of darkness. If the light that is in you is darkness, how great is that darkness! (Mt. 6:22-23)*

Our churches are not effective and our work for God is not filled with Joy and His presence because we haven't made growing in Love for God out of the knowledge of how much he loves us our reward. We have made other things the mark of success and our goal in the church, Instead of growing in the love of the Sermon on the Mount. This is what Jesus is going to call great in the kingdom of God. We have not made the Sermon on the Mount our goal in the church. We have not made the joy that comes from being faithful to steward our hearts in growing in the Love for God and for our neighbor, so that we may enter into the Joy of the Lord, our mark or goal in ministry.

What are the Ultimate Eternal Rewards

After the Sermon on the Mount is established as our mark of success and greatness in the kingdom of God, another buffer against the spirit of this world in our lives and ministries is being faithful to pursue God's assignment and calling in our lives, so as to receive eternal rewards, not temporal rewards of fame, fortune and material prosperity. Jesus taught in the parable of the talents and the faithful servant that we will be rewarded for how faithful we are over what he gave us, not what he gave someone else. This faithfulness is what we will be rewarded for:

> *25. His lord said unto him, Well done, good and faithful servant; thou hast been faithful over a few things, I will make thee ruler over many things: enter thou into the joy of thy lord. (Mat 25:23)*

Our issues of sin and immorality and falling into snares of the enemy even as we engage in religious activities of praying and participating in significant ministry are also because we don't have a revelation of eternity. We don't do ministry with eternal rewards in view. We do ministry with temporal rewards in view, which leads to fleshly pursuits and pleasures. We make our focus pleasing man and the pleasures of men and the flesh, not God and his pleasures. When we do ministry events we pray temporal prayers focused on getting God to show up for our carnal, earthly, shallow purposes. We want to be seen as significant, or we want to be fulfilled in what we are doing, or we want to please man. We don't do it to please Jesus, or to receive a reward in the next life. If we did it wouldn't matter how good we preached, whether people liked what we said, or how we said it. If we are doing it to please God, we are successful whether or not anybody else thinks highly of us or not. But because we're not looking unto Jesus who is the author and finisher of our faith our focus is people and our standing in this life. We are looking unto man, me or my authority, or my followers, to be considered legitimate, or even to be seen as being anointed, or worthy of our calling, etc, etc.

Therefore after we preach, or after we pray, or after the event we try to continuing seeking God, but because we have already received our reward (the event, the recognition, the anointing) we can't continue being faithful to him, or loving him, because our focus is temporal and temporal rewards. Our focus is on being seen in the eyes of man as great, not great in the eyes of God, which is achieved by walking in and teaching the Sermon on the Mount. This is what leads to unfaithfulness in our marriages in the church, and to our kids and most of all, unfaithfulness to Jesus. Because we are not trying to be found faithful to him, we are trying to be found faithful to what people think of us, or to what we are supposed to be in the people's eyes, not who we are in God's eyes.

Therefore our focus must be readjusted to have an eternal view, a focus on the next life, on receiving our major rewards in eternity. Our focus must be adjusted to look unto Jesus who is the author and the finisher of our faith. Our focus must be the promise being given to our children's children. Our focus must be adjusted to having our wives, husbands and children say who we are, not what men, and people that don't really know us, say who we are. Our focus must be adjusted to have Jesus say, "Well done my good and faithful servant enter into the **eternal** joys of the Lord."

The Joy Set before Us

Heb 12:2 looking unto Jesus the author and finisher of our faith; who for the joy that was set before him endured the cross, despising the shame, and is set down at the right hand of the throne of God.

To endure to the end we must keep our eyes on Jesus, looking unto Him, the author and finisher of our faith; who for the joy that was set before him endured the cross, despising the shame. This joy spoken of in this verse gives us a focus that every believer should set before their cross experience in this life to make it to the end with Jesus being our end all. As Jesus endured His cross, every believer has a cross to bear (Matt 16:21). What is that cross? I believe the cross of the believer are those things in the beatitudes that we are pressing to enter into in order to respond rightly in kingdom love - *being poor in spirit, spiritual mourning, walking in meekness, hungering for righteousness, showing mercy, embracing purity, being a peacemaker, and enduring persecution.* These beatitudes are what our cross represents. In addition to these, our cross represents our sin nature that is antithetical to these 8 beatitudes. We must overcome self to be able to endure to the end.

What is the Joy of the Lord

With that being the case, every believer must seek to know what the joy of the Lord is, and set that before us in order to endure to the end of our cross in this life. The Joy of the Lord is supposed to be our strength (Neh. 8:10), our focus, and our eternal reward that motivates us to endure to the end. What is that joy? When the scripture speaks of the joy set before Jesus, it's not speaking of an emotion, but a place. It's actually speaking of the place of communion and fellowship with the father, that's been restored to Him, that He had before He came into the world to take on the sins

190

of the world. Sin is not an act, as much as it is a place of separation from the father. Sin separates us from the father. When Jesus took on Himself the sins of the world on Calvary's Cross he was separated from His father. Hebrews 12:2 says, *"who for the joy that was set before Him endured the cross, despising the shame, **and is set down at the right hand of the throne of God."*** This joy set before Jesus was his goal and focus, to be returned to the place He had with the father before the world was. This is what enabled him to be set down at the right hand of the throne of God. This place at the right hand of the throne of God is the place of victory through intercession. It is the place of intimacy and intercession with and for God that empowers our reign in the earth. We will reign forever with Christ through intimacy and intercession, being seated with Him in heavenly places by Christ Jesus. The joy of the Lord set before him, as well as every believer, is the ministry of prayer, communion and fellowship with the father being restored to humanity with the casting down of sin and the sin nature as we receive our resurrected bodies, at the appearing of Christ to His saints.

> *1Co 15:22 For as in Adam all die, (separated from God) even so in Christ shall all be made alive.23 But every man in his own order: Christ the firstfruits; afterward they that are Christ's at his coming. 24 Then cometh the end, when he shall have delivered up the kingdom to God, even the Father; when he shall have put down all rule and all authority and power. 25 For he must reign, till he hath put all enemies under his feet.*

The goal in enduring to the end is not the prize of the thing you receive, not the reward of a corruptible crown, but what's at the end that we must make our goal and pursuit is **the joy set before us**.

> *Mat 25:21 His lord said unto him, well done, thou good and faithful servant: thou hast been faithful over a few things, I will make thee ruler over many*

things: **enter thou into the joy of thy Lord.**

The Ultimate Eternal reward is not being ruler over many things, even though that is an incentive. It's not the essence and totality of the eternal fulfillment of God's reward. It's still a temporal reward compared to the ultimate eternal reward. Increase in size of ministry, or increase in the measure of your rule is not the ultimate eternal reward that fulfills our spirits in the age to come. The ultimate eternal reward is ruling with him, not just ruling over many things. The ultimate eternal reward in the entering into of the joy of the Lord, its entering into a restored, unbroken, unceasing fellowship with the Father, ruling with Him without the hindrance or obstacles of sin, or the sin nature. Now that's something to look forward to. We know that in this life we see through a glass darkly. We only have fellowship with the father through the blood of Jesus, but in the next life we shall see him face to face as he is. At that time, Jesus says, in John 16:25;

> *These things have I spoken unto you in proverbs: but the time cometh, when I shall no more speak unto you in proverbs, but I shall shew you plainly of the Father. 26 At that day ye shall ask in my name: and I say not unto you, that I will pray the Father for you: 27 For the Father himself loveth you, because ye have loved me, and have believed that I came out from God.*

The entering into the joy of the Lord is our eternal reward, and what we should be seeking after. But we don't seek after this as an eternal incentive because we don't know what the Joy of the Lord is, and what the joy of the Lord is connected to. In scripture there are 14 instances given that show what the joy of the Lord produces and what it is connected to.

What is the Joy of the Lord

1. There is joy that a man child is birth into the world (John 17:20) - *Joy births new life.*

2. When the wise men saw the star that directed them to the Baby Jesus, the one who had been born from God the father in heaven, they rejoiced with exceeding great joy (Matt 2:10) *Joy over prophetic direction.*

3. The disciples received great joy at the revelation of the Resurrection of Jesus Christ from the dead. (Matt 28:6-8). *Joy is connected to the resurrection.*

4. When the sower sowed the word, those that received the word, received it with joy. (Matt 13:20). *Joy is connected to receiving the Word.*

5. The treasure of the kingdom of heaven, when it is found there is a joy that sells all that a man has to get that kingdom. (Matt 13:44). *Joy is connected to finding the treasure of the kingdom of heaven.*

6. Zechariah and Elizabeth were to receive joy and gladness at the birth of the prophet John. (Luke 1:14) *Joy is connected to the birthing of the prophetic.*

7. The miracle baby John received joy in the womb at the sound of the word of Mary, the carrier of the living word. (Luke 1:44) *Joy is connected to coming in contact with miracle birthings of deliverance.*

8. The shepherds receive good tidings of great joy at the announcing of the birth of Jesus. (Luke 2:10) *Joy is connected to hearing good news.*

9. Those that are persecuted are to receive joy and rejoice because of their great reward in heaven for persecution on the lines of the prophets of the O.T. (Matt 5:12) *Joy is connected to being found worthy to suffer persecution for the name of Jesus.*

10. The seventy returned with joy with the knowledge that the devils are subject them, but Jesus told them to redirect their joy to the knowledge that their names were written in the lambs book of life. (Luke 10:17) *Joy is connected to knowing that our names are written in the book of life, as we operate in power over devils in the earth.*

11. There is joy in the presence of the angels of God over one sinner that repents. (Luke 15:10) *Joy is connected to the presence of angels in heaven rejoicing over sinners on earth that repent.*

12. There was joy when Jesus gave his disciples the word of the promise of the father, to tarry in Jerusalem, until they would be endued with power, and when he lifted up his hands blessed them. (Luke 24:52) *Joy is connected to the promise of power from heaven being manifested on earth.*

13. Hearing the voice of the bridegroom brings fulfilled joy. (John 3:23) *Joy is connected to hearing the voice of the bridegroom.*

14. The hearing of the words of Jesus spoken to our spirit in the time of tribulation. (John 16:33) *Joy is connected to hearing Jesus speak during the time of tribulation.*

In each instance the Joy of the Lord is directly tied to a person, Christ Jesus or Christ-likeness being seen through the Word, or encountering the Word made flesh. The joy of the Lord comes as a result of the promise, the word, or the word manifested in the flesh to each one that loves and pursues Him as their great reward. A family, Church, ministry or business that has these standards of the Sermon on the Mount and eternal rewards of the Joy of the Lord as the mark or goal for their lives in God's kingdom will have 5 specific characteristics that are present and manifesting:

1. **A PERSONAL Prayer Life** *(Consistent personal time of prayer daily)*

2. **RIGHT RELATIONSHIPS in our Marriages and Families**. *(Prayer & devotions, quality time being kept in home)*

3. **THE WHOLE MINISTRY becoming a house of prayer,** praying thy kingdom come, thy will be done in earth as it is in heaven. *(Every member having a prayer watch and keeping it)*

4. **RIGHT SOCIAL SKILLS AND SERVICES IN THE COMMUNITY and CENTER,** *(Justice ministry being offered to the community where the ministry is located and throughout the city)*

5. **RIGHT RELATIONSHIPS WITH THE OPPOSITE SEX, RIGHT RACE RELATIONS, and socio-economic relations.** *(Sexual purity & right multi-ethnic flow in our ministries)*

For other Book Releases by Brondon Mathis:
Go to www.Amazon.com to order

1. **Upon This Rock I will Build My Church**. *The end-time purpose of the church built upon the book of the Revelation*

2. **My Home shall be called a House of Prayer.** *Our Family vision for training our children in the way they should go.*

3. **The Coming Forerunner Ministry Out of Africa -** *Africa & African America's end-time calling leading God's house of prayer to reconciliation and fullness.*

4. **My Money is Restored** - *The story of Joseph and the principles for the preparing to Arise during the coming financial fallout*

Contact info:
Brondon Mathis
614-745-9683, office
816-654-2186, cell
yeshuamovement@gmail.com
facebook/brondonmathis.com

Made in the USA
Charleston, SC
30 January 2016